YORK NOTES

General Editors: Professor A.N. Jeffares (*University of Stirling*) & Professor Suheil Bushrui (*American University of Beirut*)

V.S. Naipaul

A HOUSE FOR MR BISWAS

Notes by Rosemary Pitt

BA (DURHAM)
Lecturer in English Language and Literature, City and East London College

LONGMAN
YORK PRESS

YORK PRESS
Immeuble Esseily, Place Riad Solh, Beirut.

LONGMAN GROUP UK LIMITED
Longman House,
Burnt Mill,
Harlow,
Essex

First published 1982
Reprinted 1988

ISBN 0-582-02271-1

Produced by Longman Group (FE) Ltd
Printed in Hong Kong

ENG
R 568691K

Contents

Part 1

Introduction

The life and works of V. S. Naipaul

Vidiadhar Surajprasad Naipaul was born in 1932 at Chaguanas in central Trinidad. His grandfather, who came from a village in Uttar Pradesh in north-east India, was one of the thousands of indentured labourers who came to Trinidad from India in the last century to work on the sugar plantations. V. S. Naipaul grew up in Trinidad as part of a large family which included one brother, Shiva (who is also a novelist), five sisters, and fifty cousins. The family were Brahmins, Hindus of the highest caste and strictly orthodox, and his childhood was spent in a quasi-Indian environment. The children, however, were exposed to other influences as well; they went to schools where they mixed with negroes and Europeans, and spoke English, rather than Hindi, as their first language. Naipaul describes himself as having been 'born an unbeliever'.

In 1938 the family moved to the capital city of Trinidad, Port of Spain, and the Hindu rituals became rarer. He describes this period in the opening chapter of his novel *An Area of Darkness* and comments: 'The family life that I have been describing began to dissolve when I was six or seven; when I was fourteen it had ceased to exist'.* This dissolution is described also in *A House for Mr Biswas* through the Tulsi family. Naipaul's father was a journalist; he felt very close to him, though he described him as a 'defeated man', and he is the prototype for Mr Biswas. Like Anand, the son of Mr Biswas, Naipaul won an exhibition to Queen's Royal College in Port of Spain, and at eighteen, another scholarship from there to the University of Oxford. He was in England when his father died. After graduating with an Honours degree in English, he worked as a reviewer and in 1955 married an Englishwoman. His first novel *The Mystic Masseur* was published in 1957. He has spent much of his life travelling, returning always to London because 'it is a good place for getting lost in'. He sees himself as a man without roots; he never felt at home in Trinidad, and writes critically of it in his book of travel essays *The Middle Passage* (1962); and he was repelled by India when he visited it in 1962. In an interview that year, he said that he had

*An Area of Darkness, Penguin Books, Harmondsworth, 1964, p. 35.

never lived in any house for more than three-and-a-half years, a fact which is echoed in *A House for Mr Biswas*, and gives greater force to the latter's search for a permanent home.

His early fiction – *The Mystic Masseur* (1957), *The Suffrage of Elvira* (1958), and *Miguel Street* (1959) – is based on his childhood in Trinidad. All these tales of Trinidad Indians are light, satirical, and detached in tone. They were well-received and two won prizes, but they were also criticised for the way in which he was making fun of his own people. He retaliated in an essay by saying that none of these comments would have been made about a comic French or American novel, or an English satirical writer such as Evelyn Waugh (1903–66), and that they arose out of an ignorance of life in Trinidad without which 'it is easy for my books to be dismissed as farces and my characters as eccentrics'.* *A House for Mr Biswas*, however, which he finished writing in 1960, shows a fuller involvement with life in Trinidad, and transcends any limitations imposed by cultural barriers. His next work *The Middle Passage* (1962) is a work of non-fiction, consisting of 'Impressions of Five Societies – British, French and Dutch – in the West Indies and South America' as the sub-title tells us. It is a tour of the former slave colonies of Surinam, British Guiana, Martinique, Jamaica and Trinidad. The book shows an impatience with what Naipaul saw as the squalor, inefficiency and bigotry of the places he visited with their 'borrowed' cultures. He was praised for the lucidity with which he defined the problems of a post-colonial society, but the book made him a controversial figure. He was accused by the well-known West Indian novelist George Lamming (author of *In the Castle of My Skin*, 1953, an autobiographical account of growing up in Barbados) of writing 'castrated satire' and using satire as a refuge for a colonial writer who is 'ashamed of his cultural background'. Lamming accused him also of limiting his material too closely to the Indian segment of the population. Naipaul takes up this point in *An Area of Darkness*, when he admits that the confrontation of different communities is increasingly fundamental to the West Indian experience, but states that 'to see the attenuation of the culture of my childhood as the result of a dramatic confrontation of opposed worlds would be to distort reality. To me the worlds were juxtaposed and mutually exclusive'. He also answered the former charge by arguing in *The Middle Passage* that what the formless West Indian society needs is writers to give it shape, identity, authentic values, and a sense of direction, writers who are not afraid to employ the gifts of 'subtlety and brutality' that are required. He argues that formerly irony and satire in writing have not been acceptable since 'the insecure wish to be heroically

*'London', *The Overcrowded Baracoon*, Penguin Books, Harmondsworth, 1976, p. 11.

portrayed', and clearly he has achieved much as a writer in confirming the success of these modes of writing for portraying social comedy, as well as probing deeper issues.

His next novel, *Mr Stone and the Knight's Companion* (1963), is set in contemporary London with an English protagonist and is a richly humorous story of a clerk and his fantasies. *An Area of Darkness* (1964) returns to non-fiction, and is the record of his visit to the land of his ancestors, a visit which he felt later should not have been made since 'it had broken my life in two'. This work is of great relevance to *A House for Mr Biswas*. *The Mimic Men* (1967), his sixth novel, is an account of a West Indian political exile in London who moves between his native island of Isabella (Naipaul's name for Trinidad) and London. It is a powerful account of the two societies and of the problem of rootlessness, which is a central concern of his work. *A Flag on the Island*, a book of short stories, was also published in 1967, and was followed by Naipaul's first attempt at writing history, *The Loss of El Dorado* (1969). It is an imaginative study of 'two moments when Trinidad was touched by history'. The first is a tale of greed, the race between Raleigh and the Spaniard Berrio to discover the treasure of El Dorado; the second is the governorship of the despotic General Picton; both events suggested to Naipaul the paucity of a colonial society 'that could refer only to race and money'.

His next novel *In a Free State* (1971) deals with three main episodes concerning, firstly, an Indian servant who is transplanted from Bombay to Washington; secondly, two West Indian brothers who are moved to London; and, finally, an English man and woman who travel, or flee, through an African country. It is again a fine study of rootlessness and the meaning of freedom. A further selection of essays entitled *The Overcrowded Baracoon* was published in 1972, and has a more political emphasis than his other works with an analysis of elections in America and the West Indies. His eighth novel *Guerrillas* (1975) returns to the society of a small tropical island for its penetrating and dramatic account of political intrigue and racism, while his most recent novel *A Bend in the River* (1979) is the story of an East Indian living in an isolated outpost on the coast of Africa, who is caught up in political turmoil and eventually has to leave. Naipaul has also published two more books of essays: *India: A Wounded Civilisation* (1977), an extended study of Indian attitudes; and in 1980, *The Return of Eva Peron* which contains four previously published essays on Michael X and the Black Power Killings in Trinidad; a study of Peron's Argentina; an account of Mobutu's Zaïre; and an essay on Joseph Conrad.

The background of the novel

Trinidad

Today East Indians (a term that distinguishes them from two other types of Indians in the Caribbean islands – the American Indians, and the West Indians) comprise just over one-third of the total population of Trinidad. They are of Hindu or Moslem belief. India was the main overseas source of cheap labour after the abolition of negro slavery in 1834. No negro would work on the sugar plantations, the scenes of their slavery, and there was a steady flow of labour into the West Indies between about 1845 and 1917. Almost half the remainder of the population is composed of people of African descent, and the other half is of mixed races.

The first European to arrive in the island was Christopher Columbus, who discovered it in 1498. The first Spanish settlement was established in 1532, and the island was used mainly as a base for expeditions to the mainland in search of the fabled land of El Dorado, the subject of Naipaul's eighth novel. There was a large influx of Frenchmen in the late eighteenth century, who introduced the sugar cane. After war broke out between Spain and England in 1797, the island was captured and ceded to England in 1802. In 1962 it achieved independence within the British Commonwealth, and became a republic in 1976.

The period covered in the novel is approximately the forty-six years of Mr Biswas's life between about 1905 and 1951. The main changes which are recorded are the decline of the Hindu culture and rituals as they undergo the process of 'creolisation', and the accompanying changes in attitude. Mr Biswas himself is caught between the old culture from India and the emerging cross-fertilisations, which are shown in many ways, culminating in the departure of Mr Biswas's own children, Anand and Savi, on scholarships to study abroad. Naipaul's own views on this process, as reflected by Mr Biswas in the novel, appear to be ambivalent. He clearly regrets the passing of some of the old traditions, and satirises the new emphasis on materialism and self-advancement. In his essay on Trinidad in *The Middle Passage*, which is of great relevance to the novel, he describes Trinidad as a 'materialist immigrant society' which lacks a culture and history of its own and emphasises 'modernity' at all costs, a modernity which involves ignoring local products and using those advertised in American magazines. It is a society which admires the picaroon (from a sixteenth-century Spanish term), or rogue, illustrated in the novel by the story of Billy who cheats people of their houses. Naipaul summarises his view in his image of Trinidad as: 'A peasant-minded, money-minded community, spiritually static because cut off from its roots, its religion reduced to rites without philosophy, set in a materialist colonial society . . .'. Although this essay was written in 1962, the views he expresses in it are relevant to, and reflected in, *A House for Mr Biswas*. Naipaul is concerned primarily to describe what he sees, rather than to hanker after the past in a nostalgic way, or to offer panaceas for the future. The reader of the novel is made to sense the inevitability of progress, and this is shown as having some positive aspects. The flow of American dollars into the island, with the growing American presence there during the Second World War, brings prosperity, as well as a growing spirit of competition. It enables parents to send their children abroad to be educated. Mr Biswas fears for his son's future if the boy does not get some kind of education, but his fears are transformed into hope and optimism when his son goes abroad on a scholarship. The education system itself is viewed in an ambivalent way. It is both a progressive force and responsible for the decay of Hindu tradition. It is Mr Biswas's education which makes him think differently from his illiterate brothers and question the family structure in which he finds himself, just as it is Owad's educational superiority that automatically secures his recognition as head of the Tulsi clan. The system of education, however, with its emphasis on European topics, is shown as remote from Trinidad. Mr Biswas is taught about oases and igloos on his entry to the 'new world' at school in Pagotes, topics as removed from his experience as the comic irrelevance of the assignments he is sent by the English school of journalism. Similarly, Anand comes to see the sacred thread ceremony merely as a convenient excuse for absenting himself from school, for he and his father know that he could not present a shaved head in school without inviting ridicule from the other children and teachers. He is encouraged by Mr Biswas to spend his retreat learning school notes, and his performance of the *puja* at Shorthills is a mockery – he diverts himself by sticking flower stems under the god's chin, and cannot treat the rituals seriously. This is the world which Owad and his brother Shekhar had entered 'where education was the only protection'.

These cultural changes are reflected also in language; Hindi is seen as the language of the society into which Mr Biswas is born, but English begins to be used on public occasions, as, for instance, when Tara addresses the photographer at Raghu's funeral, and Hindi becomes the language of intimacy. Mr Biswas and Shama begin their marriage speaking in English, 'for there was as yet little friendship between them'. In the city it can be a 'secret' language, as used by the widows when they visit Mrs Tulsi's house, and the 'readers and learners' understand Hindi, but cannot speak it. Mr Biswas himself uses English at Hanuman House 'even when the other person spoke Hindi' as a gesture of rebellion and independence; and by the end of the novel it is Trinidadian Creole English which holds sway.

Although Naipaul has protested against the idea that the novel is 'documentary', stating that: 'What I would do was to write according to my imagination, and then consult people on little items of inconsequential information to lend vividness and verisimilitude to the story', the novel does record social change in a concrete and convincing way. L. White summarises it neatly:*

> by the end of the novel a whole history has passed before our eyes . . . . [Naipaul] chronicles the stages in the loss of India, the shift from country to town, from Hindi to English, from a preoccupation with Fate to a preoccupation with ambition, so that as we move from the world of Raghu to the world of Anand, we are dealing not only with the life of a man but also with the history of a culture.

Hinduism

The religion of Hinduism originated among the Aryan tribes in India. Hinduism is based chiefly on the caste system rather than on a system of beliefs or doctrines. There are five main castes, the highest of which is the Brahmin or priestly caste, to which Mr Biswas belongs. Members of this caste are treated with respect, and to be a Brahmin is a sign of great status. This is seen in the novel where Mr Biswas goes as a boy to Tara's house and is 'respected as a Brahmin and pampered'. He is dressed in a clean *dhoti*, and given a gift of money and cloth. Again, at Pundit Jairam's, he travels with him to perform the mechanical side of his offices, and, 'invested with the sacred thread and all the other badges of caste' is everywhere 'the object of regard'. The duties of a Brahmin include the performance of *puja*, or worship, which for the orthodox Hindu is centred in the home. It takes place in a room set aside for this purpose and containing a shrine, with an image of the family's chosen deity, together with other symbols of the sacred and vessels and instruments of worship such as bowls and lamps. Household worship makes use of fire for purification (a symbol of the sun); water, also for purification; food-offerings; incense; flowers; and coloured powders for ornamentation. It is carried out at certain fixed times: sunrise, midday and sunset. When worshipping, the orthodox Hindu will be dressed in the traditional way, wearing the sacred thread, and caste or sect marks on the forehead and sometimes the arms and other parts of the body. Certain sacraments also take place, and are usually four in number: birth, initiation, marriage, and death. The ceremony of initiation plays some part in the novel when Anand, despite his distaste for religious ritual, becomes attracted by this ceremony which most of his male cousins have experienced. It involves being invested with the sacred thread and going into retreat to study and learn secret verses. Its main attraction for Anand is the shaving of the head. He asks for a print of the goddess Lakshmi to be hung on the wall of his room to whom he says his prayers, but this worship soon ends when his main motive for undergoing the ceremony – to miss school – is thwarted when Mr Biswas arranges for it to take place during the long summer holiday. The sacrament of death should take place on the bank of a sacred river, and following the death, the corpse should be carried to a sacred spot to be cremated. In the case of Mr Biswas, the cremation takes place on the banks of a muddy stream.

Hinduism also figures largely in the novel as forming part of Mr Biswas's campaign against the Tulsis when he joins a breakaway movement of protestant Hindu missionaries who had come from India and adopted the ancient name of 'Aryans'. They preach that caste is unimportant, that Hinduism should accept converts, that idols should be abolished, and that women should be educated, thus 'preaching against all the doctrines the orthodox Tulsis held dear'. Mr Biswas is impressed by the speeches of the leader, Pankaj Rai, and finds himself agreeing with the ideas that idols were an insult to the human intelligence and to God, and that a man's caste should be determined only by his actions, a point which seems to be proved by his brother-in-law Ramchand whose clean and comfortable hut 'indicated lowness in no way'. Pankaj Rai is soon discredited and his place taken by Shivlochan, BA., and the movement seems to disintegrate amidst arguments about the relative virtues of peaceful persuasion or militant conversion. However, Mr Biswas continues to be influenced by his Hindu background, as we see when, for example, he recites the words 'Rama Rama' as protection during the storm at Green Vale, and Hinduism is a vital and integral part of the novel.

A note on the text

A House for Mr Biswas was first published by André Deutsch, London, in 1961. The Penguin paperback edition, Penguin Books, Harmondsworth, 1969, is referred to in these Notes.

Part 2

Summaries
of A HOUSE FOR MR BISWAS

A general summary

Mohun Biswas is a Trinidadian Indian who dies at the age of forty-six in a house in Port of Spain where he has been living with his wife and four children. He was born in a country village, surrounded by ill omens. His family is scattered after his father's death and he moves with his mother to Pagotes. At school he discovers a talent for lettering, and later becomes a sign-writer. Initially, however, he is sent by his aunt Tara to the household of a pundit to learn to be a Hindu priest; but he leaves in disgrace after eight months and works in a rum shop run by Tara's drunken brother-in-law. After being wrongfully accused of stealing he joins a former schoolfriend in the sign-writing business, in the course of which he goes to Hanuman House, the home of the Tulsis. He is then trapped into promising to marry Shama, the sixteen-year-old daughter of Mrs Tulsi, as he is of the right Hindu caste. No dowry is offered and he is expected to join the family workforce by working on the land with the other husbands. He immediately rebels, but without any money or position of his own he finds himself dependent on the Tulsi household from then until shortly before his death. After successfully disrupting the smooth running of the house, Mr Biswas is sent to a small rural village, The Chase, to act as manager of a Tulsi food shop. During the six years he spends there with his growing family, the shop continually loses money, and his family spend an increasing amount of time at Hanuman House. Finally he joins them there, and is then sent to Green Vale to act as overseer for Mrs Tulsi's powerful brother-in-law. He is wholly unsuited to such work and feels persecuted by the labourers under him.

He suffers a mental breakdown and has to return to Hanuman House to convalesce after a storm destroys the ramshackle house he has built. Forced to earn his living again, he leaves the Tulsis and goes to stay with his sister and her husband in Port of Spain. He finds work as a journalist on the *Sentinel* newspaper, and this leads to a reconciliation with the Tulsis. He goes to live with his family at Mrs Tulsi's house in the city which she shares with her younger son, Owad, until he is sent abroad to study medicine.

Mr Biswas takes a growing interest in the education of his son Anand and a close relationship develops between them. Meanwhile the Tulsis move to an estate at Shorthills and Mr Biswas is persuaded to join them. The Tulsi family begins to disintegrate under new social and economic pressures, and Mr Biswas leaves after the house he builds there is destroyed by a fire. He returns to Mrs Tulsi's crowded house in the city and remains there until he moves to his own house in Sikkim Street after a fierce quarrel with Mrs Tulsi and Owad. His job at the *Sentinel* has changed to that of social investigator of 'Deserving Destitutes' which leads to a new lease of life when he is given a government post in a Social Welfare Department. His hopes, however, increasingly centre on Anand, who wins an exhibition to the prestigious Queen's College in the city. The house in Sikkim Street leads Mr Biswas into heavy debt, especially as it is over-priced and in need of major repairs, but he is overjoyed at possessing his own house and land.

After the government department is disbanded, he returns to the *Sentinel* until put on half-pay when he develops heart-trouble and is eventually dismissed. Anand is now studying at university in England and does not return during his father's illness, but his daughter, Savi, returns and gets a well-paid job. Mr Biswas then dies suddenly and receives a traditional Hindu cremation, after which his wife and children return to the empty house.

Detailed summaries

Prologue

Mr Biswas is dismissed from his job at the *Sentinel* ten weeks before his death. Neither he nor his wife have any money to pay the mortgage on the house, but he is comforted by his wife's efforts to help him instead of returning to her family and by the wonder and triumph of having acquired his own house where he can wander freely and feel secure. The house was bought from a corrupt solicitor's clerk who had concealed its shoddiness and makeshift design from the eager Mr Biswas. As soon as he and his wife Shama (who had shown hostility to the idea and had refused to look at the house) move in, they discover all the defects in its structure and layout; but they adapt to these quickly, and it seems to Mr Biswas – on his first return from hospital – a welcoming and ready-made world.

COMMENTARY: This introduction reports the death of the novel's main character, Mr Biswas; thus we know that the main body of the novel will trace his life up to this point, and while the element of surprise is taken away by knowing of the death, Naipaul is free to use a variety of stylistic devices such as flashback scenes depicting events prior to the narrative and prediction of future events, which involve us closely in Mr Biswas's life. We are also informed of how much the house matters to Mr Biswas as a symbol of his freedom and independence.

NOTES AND GLOSSARY:

big-shot: a successful business man

the *Meditations* of Marcus Aurelius: Marcus Aurelius was Roman Emperor from AD161 to AD180; he believed in the philosophy of Stocism which preached that virtue is the aim of life and that the passions and appetites should be rigidly subdued

Deserving Destitutes: people living without the basic necessities and deserving support

unaccommodated: the final word of the prologue is an echo of Shakespeare's tragedy *King Lear* (III.4), when Lear, on seeing the beggar, Poor Tom, on the heath, says: 'Unaccommodated man is no more but such a poor, bare, forked animal as thou art'

PART 1

Chapter 1: Pastoral

Mr Biswas was born away from his father's village in the hut belonging to his grandmother Bissoondaye. He is born the wrong way round, at midnight, and with six fingers, all of which are seen as portents of ill-luck and disaster. The pundit also predicts that the boy will be a lecher and a spendthrift because of his widely spaced teeth, and that he should be kept away from trees and water. He will also have an unlucky sneeze, as happens on the occasion of his father's drowning in the pond.

After his father's death the family have to leave, and thus Mr Biswas escapes the expected course of events. This would have meant his remaining illiterate and working as a grass-cutter in the fields, perhaps saving enough money to rent or buy a few acres of land where he could plant his own sugar canes. This is a path which his brother Pratap follows; he even becomes prosperous, with a house of his own. Tara, his mother's sister, comes to organise his father's funeral, and takes his sister, Dehuti, to live with her. His mother, Bipti, leaves her village after her garden is ransacked by some neighbours who mistakenly believe that her husband, who was thought to be the richest man in the village, had buried bags of money there. She takes Mr Biswas with her to the town of Pagotes, where they live as dependent relations of Tara in a back street. The two brothers are sent to Felicity to work on the sugar estates and Mr Biswas, who finds himself increasingly distant from his mother, feels isolated and alone.

COMMENTARY: The first words spoken in this chapter, which refer to Fate and how people cannot fight it, summarise neatly the attitude of the older generation of Indian Hindus from which Mr Biswas descends. He differs radically from them, however, in that he attempts to determine the course of his life himself in an active way, despite all the ill omens and pessimism expressed at his birth. The value of homes and houses is also emphasised in the final paragraph, since we are told that Mr Biswas is now leaving 'the only house to which he had some right' and will be a 'wanderer' for the next thirty-five years without a house of his own, and his only family will be the Tulsis with their 'engulfing world'.

NOTES AND GLOSSARY:

pundit:	a Hindu learned in the Sanskrit language, and the science, laws and religion of India
almanac:	a register of the dates of the year, including predictions about the future
milkmaids ... Lord Krishna:	Krishna, the Hindu god of fire and light; according to Hindu legend he was a brave, beautiful youth brought up by cowherds, and had love-affairs with the milkmaids
the Shiva dance:	Shiva is the third deity in the Hindu trinity, representing the destructive principle in life, but also a restoring or renovating power; also the God of Dance
dhoti:	loin-cloth
carried weight:	was considered influential
sabots:	wooden shoes
roti:	a pancake
piquet:	picket; a stake or peg
hibiscus:	a shrub with large red or pink flowers
calabash:	the shell of a gourd used as a drinking vessel or domestic utensil
henna:	a dye
chock up:	to wedge in order to prevent slipping
eczema:	a skin disease
maharajin:	the wife of a *maharaja*, the title assumed by some Indian princes

Chapter 2: Before the Tulsis

No traces remain of Mr Biswas's birthplace, although the land his mother once owned later yields oil, and the swamp region becomes a garden city. Even his birth certificate has to be invented and drawn up by a Muslim solicitor, F. Z. Ghany. At the mission school he is taught by Lal, a converted Hindu, and learns many useless facts. He befriends Alec, who shocks the school by taking Dodd's Kidney Pills and passing blue urine. They keep their home lives secret, partly because Mr Biswas is not happy there and still views it as a temporary arrangement. He feels detached from his brothers, now grown men, and only sees his sister when taking part in a religious ceremony at his aunt's house, where he is respected as a Brahmin and treated with honour. He also goes there to read to his uncle Ajodha from 'That Body of Yours'. After six years Mr Biswas is taken away from school, and goes to live with pundit Jairam where he learns religious ceremonies, including the morning prayer ceremony, or *puja*. Two episodes discredit him – one when he steals two bananas, and the other when he defiles the sacred oleander tree with his soiled handkerchief. He returns to his mother in Pagotes, an incident he later romanticises in a poem; but he is soon sent to the sordid rum shop where he rebels against uncle Bhandat's mean and suspicious nature by spitting in the rum when he bottles it. He leaves (after a violent scene where he is accused of stealing money) determined to establish his independence and get his own job and house. During his hunt for a job he visits Dehuti and her husband Ramchand, Tara's disgraced yard boy; although he feels very separate from his sister, he is impressed that their hut is clean and comfortable with no signs of Ramchand's lower caste. A meeting with Alec then leads to his job as sign-writer. He escapes into novels in search of romance, and identifies with the heroes of Samuel Smiles. Finally his search takes him to Hanuman House in Arwacas.

NOTES AND GLOSSARY:

Raleigh's dream:	Sir Walter Raleigh (*c.*1552–1618), the English explorer, soldier and poet, searched in vain for gold in South America
oil derricks:	the structures built over oil wells
Presbyterianism:	Protestant Christian religion tracing its origin to Calvinism
affidavit:	a voluntary affirmation sworn before a person qualified to administer an oath
tamarind rod:	a stick made from the branch of a tamarind tree
bodice:	a type of vest

leg-of-mutton sleeves: sleeves in the shape of a leg of mutton

drugstore: a chemist's shop, often selling a variety of items in addition to the chemist's traditional wares

Bell's Standard Elocutionist: a manual on elocution practice, first published 1860, with a large collection of pieces of poetry and prose for recitation

Ramayana: an ancient Indian epic poem which tells of the exploits of the god Rama

sacred thread: the *upavita*, worn by upper-caste members according to Hindu custom; it is a cotton thread of three strands, which a guru gives to a boy at his initiation ceremony between the ages of eight and twelve

tulsi: a species of the herb basil, sacred to the Hindu god Vishnu

bicarbonate of soda: a powder used to cure indigestion

puja: Hindu ceremony of worship

Sanskrit: the ancient language of the Hindu sacred writings

marigolds, zinnias, oleanders: flowers which grow locally

allegory: a narrative in which the ideas and characters portrayed also refer to wider, abstract concepts; an extended metaphor

dry goods shop: shop selling clothes, drapery and so forth, as distinguished from a grocery

rock cakes: hard buns containing currants

in two twos: in a few moments

Hall Caine: Sir Thomas Henry Hall Caine (1853–1931), an English novelist who wrote *The Manxman* (1894)

Marie Corelli: an English romantic novelist (1855–1924)

Samuel Smiles: a political philisopher (1812–1904) who wrote *Self-help* (1859) and *Duty* (1880), preaching the virtues of thrift and hard work

Amerindian: a contraction of 'American-Indian'

Chapter 3: The Tulsis

Hanuman House, and the reputation of the Tulsis among Hindus, are described in detail. They are respected, though little is known about them. Mr Biswas passes a note to Shama and is called to an interview with her mother and uncle Seth. He is found to be a suitable husband and surprises himself by agreeing to marry Shama. After the ceremony he begins to think of escape; he is appalled at the hierarchical organisation of the house where the daughters' husbands' names are forgotten and they are expected to become simply Tulsis. He rebels and returns to Pagotes. Here, however, he finds that he has achieved new status with his relations and starts to accept his role, and soon returns to the Tulsi house to find that he is seen there now as troublesome, disloyal and untrustworthy. His invective against the Tulsis, particularly the 'little gods', develops into a campaign against them. He becomes involved with a breakaway Hindu movement and satirises the Tulsis for being false Hindus by sending their sons to a Roman Catholic college. The confrontation comes to a head when Mr Biswas refuses the offering at the *puja* and then spills a plateful of food on Shama's brother Owad. He is attacked by her brother-in-law Govind, and then ordered by Seth to leave.

NOTES AND GLOSSARY:

monkey-god Hanuman: a character in the *Ramayana*, worshipped as a deity in India

the Mutiny: a rising (1837–9) among Indian regiments in British service in north and central India

Punch: the famous puppet of Punch and Judy shows

prognathous: with projecting jaws

vogue: fashionable success

bluchers: old-fashioned low boots

topee: a sun-hat

creole: a descendant of European settlers in the West Indies

mango: a tropical fruit

a real gum-pot: a difficult situation

brain-feeding meals . . . fish: fish has a high protein content

hartshorn: smelling salts

Liniment: a liquid preparation for rubbing on bruises or sores

buffoon: a comic figure or fool

BA LL B: degrees of batchelor of arts, bachelor of laws

spouses: husbands or wives

cat-in-bag: an arranged marriage

a republic: a country without a monarch or absolute ruler

a serpent: a betrayer

***Discourses* of Epictetus:** Epictetus (AD55–135) was a Greek stoic philosopher

doodling: drawing figures in a casual manner

salmon only on Good Friday: in imitation of the Roman Catholic custom

a flambeau: a torch

Chapter 4: The Chase

Mr Biswas moves to this isolated village to manage a small food shop, a venture which is destined to fail from the beginning as there is a large number of such shops. To Mr Biswas his stay there seems always 'temporary and not quite real', a preparation for real life elsewhere. The shop is Tulsi property; the house is blessed by brother-in-law Hari at Shama's insistence. Even his daughter, Savi, is named by Seth and Hari, and is seen as a Tulsi. The decline of the business is furthered by Mr Biswas's attempt through the corrupt lawyer, Seebaran, to regain lost credit. He himself gets into debt as a result. He finds he has aged during these six years of boredom and futility, but he remains optimistic that 'some nobler purpose awaited him', and consoles himself with religion and philosophy, painting foreign landscapes and indulging in eccentric habits. A son is born and his family spend more time away at Hanuman House. He wins acceptance there as a person skilled in wit and argument and views it as a sanctuary from the impersonal outer world. At the same time he resents its hold over his family, and when Shama declares she wants to return there for good, they quarrel frequently until he hits her. He does not see her until their third child is born, when he too leaves The Chase and joins her at Hanuman House, staying there until he is given work on the estate at Green Vale.

COMMENTARY: This chapter highlights Mr Biswas's growing fear of the future as a blankness and an empty space, a void into which he is falling, which develops into the breakdown at Green Vale. The fear is also linked with the recurring image of the boy standing outside a lonely country hut at evening which he had seen years earlier. In spite of this feeling of emptiness, however, the period at The Chase is also a time of acquiring possessions and leaving marks of habitation.

NOTES AND GLOSSARY:

kerosene: oil used for burning in lamps

Maharajah of Barrackpore: a rich Indian prince

Workmen's Compensation Act: a law by which workmen would be paid extra money for dangerous work

Bonne Esperance: (*French*) high hopes

the calling name: name by which she would normally be addressed

Hindus ... wouldn't keep pigs: pigs are considered unclean by Hindus

telescoped: compressed, made smaller

Cydrax: a drink made from apples

poui: a sturdy creeper with a thick trailing stem, often used as a pot scourer

Alexander:	possibly Alexander the Great (356–323BC), who achieved the expansion of Greek civilisation to the east
Carnival:	annual celebration with dance and music
iconoclasm:	attack on established opinions
irreligiosity:	Christmas is a Christian festival and is not therefore usually celebrated by Hindus
cheelum:	pipe
a dose of licks:	a beating
febrifuges:	medicines to reduce fever

Chapter 5: Green Vale

Mr Biswas moves into a small room in the barracks in the damp and shadowed vale. Being largely ignorant of sugar cane and estate work, he is scorned by the labourers who fear only Seth. He wishes to move into his own house, but Seth's promises to build him one are never carried out. His frustration at the sordid surroundings and fear of the workers are expressed at first in abuse of the Tulsis to Shama, who again retreats to Hanuman House, and then in solitary periods in his room. Shortly after Christmas he visits his children, taking a large doll's house to Savi, which is subsequently destroyed by Shama because of the disruption and jealousy it arouses.

He takes Savi to live with him for a week to 'claim' her; his wife returns briefly but becomes pregnant again, and he is left essentially alone. In an attempt 'to arrest his descent into the void' Mr Biswas employs an incompetent carpenter to build a house, despite having little money to finance it. He becomes increasingly disturbed and restless and finds the objects in his room threatening, as well as the people he encounters. During a visit by his family he again hits Shama, who is pregnant, saying that she and the Tulsis are trying to kill him. She leaves, but his son, Anand, asks to stay. They move to the one finished room of the house, where the killing of Mr Biswas's dog is followed by a fierce storm and the climax of Mr Biswas's fears that 'they' are coming to destroy him. The house itself is struck by lightning.

NOTES AND GLOSSARY:

Northumberland:	a county in north-east England
emporium:	a large shop
laxly:	not strictly orthodox
felo-de-se:	self-inflicted murder
fob:	pocket for holding a watch
bower:	shady retreat

punch:	a paunch, stomach bulge
Sanatogen:	a vitamin tonic drink
euphemism:	a way of expressing something offensive in an indirect and softened manner
puss-puss:	malicious gossip
galvanize:	iron coated with zinc
dock:	reduce
Tarzan:	the hero of a series of popular stories by Edgar Rice Burroughs (1875–1950); Tarzan is a particularly strong and agile man, leading a primitive life in the jungle, and the subject of many fantastic adventures

The Hunchback of Notre Dame: popular novel (1831) by the French writer Victor Hugo (1802–85). The main characters are Esmeralda and Quasimodo, the hunchback

the wood was cured: the wood had been treated or seasoned to prevent shrinking

Coppernickus and Galilyo: Copernicus (1473–1543) was a Polish astronomer who advanced the theory that the earth and other planets revolve around the sun; Galileo (1564–1642) was the brilliant Italian scientist and astronomer who supported the Copernican theory and claimed that the earth was round

Rama Rama Sita Rama: an incantation inspired by the epic Hindu poem the *Ramayana*; Sita was the bride of Rama

---

Chapter 6: A Departure

Mr Biswas and Anand are taken back to Hanuman House. Mr Biswas gradually recovers and is able to piece together the past with its memories of horror. He is relieved to hear that the house has been burnt down completely by the labourers, thus freeing him from the past memories. He reviews his situation, reflecting that his position is still that of someone without a vocation or reliable means of supporting his family and that he would not be missed. He determines to establish his independence and feels that 'real' life with its 'especial sweetness' is still waiting for him to discover it.

NOTES AND GLOSSARY:

Ovaltine:	the brand-name of a malt-based drink, made with hot milk, and which is supposed to induce sleep
thaumaturge:	worker of miracles
aloe:	a plant used as a drug
chamar-**caste-type:**	a low-born person

PART 2

Chapter 1: 'Amazing Scenes'

Mr Biswas takes a bus to Port of Spain where he stays for a time with his sister and her husband. He feels stimulated and excited by the city, but wearies of his freedom, and the spasms of fear return. After an abortive visit to a medical specialist he recognises that he has to accept the past as a vital part of himself, and this restores the 'wholeness' of his mind. He also recognises that the spasms of fear on seeing people were caused by regret, envy, and despair, rather than fear. He acts decisively and gains a job writing on the *Sentinel* newspaper under Mr Burnett where his talent for fantasy and facetious, humorous writing gains expression. As a shipping reporter he feels in contact with different parts of the world. He is reunited with his family and sees his fourth child, and as the climax of his current good luck, is given rooms in Mrs Tulsi's house in Port of Spain. His friendship with Owad develops and he establishes a closer and more disciplined relationship with his children, involving himself also in their education. He takes a short-lived writing course from London on journalism, and invents stories with a fantasy heroine entitled 'Escape'. He plants rose-bushes in the garden and begins to think of the house as his own. This order is disturbed by news of Owad being sent to England to study medicine, and Anand's near-drowning at the docks.

COMMENTARY: The first, macabre stories Mr Biswas writes for the *Sentinel* reflect his guilt and anxiety about leaving his family, and also his feelings of insecurity and anxiety are given expression in the report of the Scarlet Pimpernel (his assumed name as he tours the island) spending the night in a tree.

NOTES AND GLOSSARY:

'Amazing Scenes': this phrase comes from one of the newspapers in the barracks room at Green Vale

brain fag: mental exhaustion

elided: omitting syllables in words

***Tom Sawyer* and *Huckleberry Finn*:** popular adventure novels by the American author Mark Twain (pen name of Samuel Clemens, 1835–1910)

***in extremis*:** at the point of death

Bonny Baby Competition: a contest to find the most attractive baby

photographs of Adolf Hitler: this dates this period in the novel as the 1930s with the beginnings of Hitler's rise to power in Nazi Germany

Scarlet Pimpernel: taken from the romantic novel of that title (1905), by Baroness Orczy (1865–1947), in which the leader of the League of the Scarlet Pimpernel, a band of young Englishmen pledged to rescue the innocent victims of the Reign of Terror in Paris after the French Revolution, outwits his opponents by means of ingenious disguises

crook: a criminal

aspirations: social ambitions

Macaulay: Thomas Babington Macaulay (1800–59), English statesman, poet and historian

eviction notice: order to leave a property

Guy Fawkes Night: annual festival celebrating the discovery of the 'Gunpowder Plot' in England in 1605 – a Roman Catholic conspiracy to murder King James I and members of parliament; Guy Fawkes, one of the conspirators, was arrested before the explosion could be detonated and the plot was foiled

Evening Standard ... *Country Life*: British daily newspapers and magazines of the period

Warwick Deeping: a popular English novelist (1877–1950)

Prince of Wales: title given to the eldest son of the King, or Queen, of England

H.E.: His Excellency (used ironically here to refer to 'the boss')

Shirley Temple: a Hollywood film actress, especially famous for the parts she played as a child

Life: an illustrated American magazine

Halévy's *History of the English People*: Halévy (1870–1937) was a French historian

---

Chapter 2: The New Régime

The house feels empty, as if awaiting change. Disaffections spread at Hanuman House as Mrs Tulsi ceases to control it effectively, and internal quarrels develop. The *Sentinel*'s tone of frivolity becomes inappropriate with the approach of war and Mr Burnett is sacked. The new editorial policy demands a strict adherence to fact, which Mr Biswas finds sterile and unrewarding. He fears for his job also, sensing that his work is mediocre. Prices rise with the impact of the war and the quality of food declines. The quarrels with Shama, and his sense of being trapped, intensify, and the sense of expectation he had of the city and his life there disappears. Anand's life of study in the exhibition class is also taxing. The destruction of the rose garden by Seth to provide space for his lorries provokes a violent scene in which Mr Biswas damages some of the furniture in the house.

NOTES AND GLOSSARY:

Spain: a reference to the Spanish Civil War (1936–9) in which General Franco and the Right Wing fought against the Republicans

MBE, OBE, CBE: Member, Order, and Commander of the British Empire; decorations awarded by the King or Queen of England

a capitalist rag: a newspaper which has profit as its chief aim

sell . . . like hot cakes: sell quickly and successfully

Dickens: Charles Dickens (1812–70), famous English novelist, noted in particular for his compassionate portrayals of the conditions of the poor

the sack: losing his job

Lamb's *Tales from Shakespeare*: Charles Lamb (1775–1834), an English essayist, adapted Shakespeare's plays for children

Lakshmi: Hindu goddess of beauty, wealth and pleasure who appears in the *Ramayana*

rakshas: evil spirits of Hindu legend who haunt cemeteries and devour human beings

jackasses: fools

Chapter 3: The Shorthills Adventure

The Tulsis leave Arwacas for a new estate in the mountains north-east of Port of Spain. Hanuman House is full of talk of the glories of the estate with its lush landscape and Shama wants to be part of the adventure. Mr Biswas consents to move there after he visits it with Mrs Tulsi and is attracted by the idea of building his own house there and living cheaply. Shorthills represents for him an adventure, an interlude, and he remains detached from its declining fortunes, since his job gives him independence and he is able to plunder the land and exploit the philosophy of 'every man for himself'. For the children it means a nightmare existence with the problems of travel to school, and shortages of food. The death of Hari is followed by that of Padma, and it seems that that family has lost its cohesive power of virtue. Mr Biswas decides to build his own house and withdraw, despite the isolation of the site. He invites his mother for a visit and she helps to clear the ground for the firing. It is this event which leads to the destruction of Mr Biswas's third house by fire. His rivalry with another brother-in-law, an ambitious extrepreneur, begins at Shorthills. Mr Biswas calls him 'W. C. Tuttle', this being the name of the author of his large collection of books, labelled by Mr Biswas as 'trash'. Their rooms are opposite to each other.

NOTES AND GLOSSARY:

'The Emperor's New Clothes':	the well-known children's story by Hans Christian Anderson (1805–75) about an emperor who, tricked by the flattery of two rogues pretending to be tailors, appeared naked in public in the belief that he wore a suit of cloth so fine that only the wisest could see it
Oliver Twist:	central character in the novel of that name (1837–8) by Dickens, dealing with the poor in workhouses and London criminals
Romain Rolland:	French essayist and novelist (1866–1944) who believed in faith in humanity based on a pantheistic religion
Boots:	famous chain of chemist shops which used to have a lending library and sell books
W. C. Tuttle:	Wilbur Coleman Tuttle (b.1883), author of over fifty popular novels about the American 'Wild West', the first of which was published in 1920
dicky seat:	an open seat behind the body of the motor-car
suttee:	a Hindu custom by which the widow was burnt on the funeral pyre with her dead husband

Chapter 4: Among the Readers and Learners

Transport becomes impossible and Mr Biswas moves back to two rooms in Mrs Tulsi's house in Port of Spain, along with the Tuttles, Govind and Chinta, and the widow, Basdai. A comic rivalry ensues over possessions, and the crowds and noise, increased by Basdai's schoolchildren boarders from Shorthills, drive Mr Biswas to walk in the streets and to see his office as a haven. He feels he is excluded from the growing prosperity in the island and fears for Anand's future job prospects as involving only 'intrigue, humiliation and dependence'. He is appointed investigator for the Deserving Destitutes Fund, and is exposed constantly to failure and misery, as well as requests for help from the widows and Bhandat. He continues to visit Ajodha and becomes friendly with Jagdat, Bhandat's son; but there is much hostility between Ajodha and his two nephews. The internal rivalries in the house preoccupy him, including that between Anand and Vidiadhar, who are both in the exhibition class. Anand's schooling and personality are described fully with the build-up to the vital examination, which he passes with great success. Mr Biswas's mother dies, and he commemorates her in an embarrassingly emotional prose poem which he writes for the literary group he has joined. He also writes a long letter to the doctor who delayed in signing her death certificate, and is rewarded by his letter being sent back and so acknowledged.

COMMENTARY: Mr Biswas destroys his fantasy 'Escape' stories with their barren heroines when confronted with the sorded realites of Bhandat's lodging where he vilifies his Chinese mistress as an 'awkward barren cow'. This can be seen as part of Mr Biswas's acceptance of the life around him and his past, though it could be seen also as a gesture of defeat and pessimism.

NOTES AND GLOSSARY:

Ella Wheeler Wilcox: an American poet and journalist (1850–1919), very popular in her day

Edward Carpenter: an English poet and writer (1844–1929) with strongly socialist views

Lorca: Federico Garcia Lorca (1898–1936), Spanish poet and playwright, assassinated at the beginning of the Spanish Civil War

Eliot: T. S. Eliot (1888–1965), a major English poet

Auden: W. H. Auden (1907–73), an English poet linked particularly with the 1930s

pomme cithère: (*French*) 'apple of Cythera'. Cythera is an island off the coast of the Peloponnese, dedicated to the Greek goddess of love, Aphrodite. The term *pomme cithère*, or love apple, can refer to a tomato

bois-canot: (*French*) a hard wood used for boat-building (*bois* means wood; *canot* means a small, open boat)

homilies: sermons or moral lessons

Jesse James and *The Return of Frank James*: American Western films based on famous bandits of the nineteenth century

Henry Fonda, Brian Donlevy, Tyrone Power: famous film stars in Hollywood during the 1940s and 1950s

ghee: oil made from butter

Measure for Measure: a play (1604) by Shakespeare (1564–1616) which centres upon the question of the nature of justice

the *Gita*:	an abbreviation for the *Bhagavadgita*, part of a famous epic poem of ancient India called the *Mahabharata*
P. G. Wodehouse:	English writer (1881–1975) of comic novels about upper class characters
The Talisman:	a historical novel (1825) by Sir Walter Scott (1771–1832)

Chapter 5: The Void

Mr Biswas involves himself closely in Anand's work at the college, and looks to his son increasingly as embodying his hopes for the future. He even loses his vision of possessing his own house again and feels much despair. A new job in a government social welfare department, however, gives him a fresh interest and sense of security. He earns extra money and has the luxury of a holiday in North Trinidad, as well as new clothes and a new car which he enjoys showing off. He feels his luck is too good to last as the department comes increasingly under attack. The Tuttles leave for their own house and the ailing Mrs Tulsi returns and exerts her tyrannies until revived by preparations for the return of Owad. Mr Biswas has to move temporarily to a tenement, and re-visits Hanuman House. The family then return to one room in Mrs Tulsi's house.

NOTES AND GLOSSARY:

yogi:	a devotee of yoga, a Hindu system of meditation often involving the practice of physical exercises
copra industry:	copra is the dried kernels of coconuts, which yield oil
Pro Bono Publico:	(*Latin*) for the public good
Caramba! ... tarde:	(*Spanish*) Heavens above! It's three o'clock already. Where is your father? Lena, go and call him. Come on, come on! We're already late
Sindhis:	people from the province of Sind in India

Chapter 6: The Revolution

Owad returns to a full house, 'like an old Hanuman House festival'. He is recognised as the new head of the family. His exploits are recounted endlessly, together with his glorification of Russia and anticipation of the socialist revolution in Trinidad. A strong antagonism develops, however, between Anand and Owad after a quarrel, and Mr Biswas 'gives notice' after a breach with Mrs Tulsi. His meeting with the solicitor's clerk in a café leads to a visit to the house in Sikkim Street which at first seems inaccessible, though most desirable. The sale of the house at Shorthills makes the price of five thousand dollars less prohibitive and he goes ahead with the purchase, in spite of Shama's disapproval, after borrowing four thousand dollars from Ajodha. Owad spends more time away from home at his brother Shekhar's house – Shekhar has married a Presbyterian, Dorothy, who upsets the Tulsis – and with medical colleagues. Talk of the revolution now ceases.

NOTES AND GLOSSARY:

Robert Taylor:	Hollywood film actor (1911–69)
Russell:	Bertrand Russell (1872–1970), distinguished modern English philosopher
Joad:	Cyril Joad (1891–1958), modern philosopher and broadcaster
Rhadakrishnan:	Sarvepalli Radhakrishnan (1888–1975), Indian philosopher, scholar and statesman
Laski:	Harold Laski (1893–1950), English political scientist
Menon:	Krishna Menon (1897–1974), an Indian nationalist and champion of India's anti-colonialist movement
solecisms:	deviations from correct grammer or idiom
Molotov:	Vyacheslav Molotov (b.1890) one of Stalin's closest advisers during the period of the purges in the 1930s in the USSR; he was Commissioner for Foreign Affairs 1939–49 and 1953–6
the Red Army:	the Soviet Army which captured Berlin in 1945
Winston Churchill's Fulton speech:	Winston Churchill (1874–1965) was the British Conservative Prime Minister (1940–5 and 1951–5) especially associated with Britain's victory in the Second World War (1939–45). The Fulton Speech he made in 1946 is often seen as the open declaration of the Cold War; he coined the phrase 'the Iron Curtain'
Maurice Thorez:	French politician (1900–64), leader of the French Communist party at this period
Rokossovsky:	Konstantin Konstantinovich Rokossovsky (1896–1968), a Marshal of the Soviet Union. During the Second World War he commanded the forces that defended Stalingrad and Moscow and led the Soviet Armies through Poland. Served as Minister of Defence in Poland (1949–56) and Deputy Minister of Defence in Soviet Union (1956–8)

Coca-cola-Kowsky: a fictitious name, or pun on the above reference, to show how ugly Mr Biswas thinks Russian names are

Joseph Dugashvili: the real name of Stalin (1879–1953). The name 'Stalin', which means 'man of steel', was his revolutionary name

Gogol: Nikolai Vasilyevich Gogol (1809–52), Russian dramatist and novelist. His novels are considered to form the foundations of the nineteenth-century tradition of Russian realism

story by a French writer: a reference to the short story 'The Necklace' by Guy de Maupassant (1850–93)

Picasso, Chagall, Rouault, Braque, Matisse: famous European painters of the twentieth century

The Moon and Sixpence: film based on a novel by William Somerset Maugham (1874–1965) which dealt with the life of the post-impressionist painter Paul Gauguin

Punch, Illustrated London News: English magazines dealing with current events

Morning Glory: a climbing plant

Chapter 7: The House

The deficiencies of the new house are soon revealed, as well as the financial commitments it involves, and Mr Biswas abuses the clerk as a crook and jerry-builder, a description which is confirmed by his elderly neighbour. The Tuttles visit, however, and are easily deceived and impressed by the house, and its inconveniences are rapidly forgotten. The yard is expanded and a garden planted.

COMMENTARY: This chapter repeats and expands several points which were made in the prologue, but here the emphasis is on the importance of the house to the children, especially Anand, as providing a stable focus for their lives and a fixed point around which their memories of childhood can be organised.

NOTES AND GLOSSARY:

jerry-builder: a builder who erects houses quickly and in a makeshift manner

---

Epilogue

Owad marries Dorothy's Presbyterian cousin and establishes a private practice in San Fernando. The Community Welfare Department is abolished with the new urge to self-improvement brought about by the war and the American influence. Mr Biswas returns to the *Sentinel*, but finds the work tedious and feels increasingly burdened by his debts. Savi and Anand go abroad on scholarships, and Mr Biswas receives unhappy and worrying letters from his son which he responds to with long humorous letters of his own. His sense of waiting for events to happen (in this case the return of his children) intensifies. He suddenly suffers a heart attack and spends a month in hospital, after which he is put on half-pay by the paper. He grows lethargic and irritable, and is sacked after spending more time in hospital. The return of Savi compensates in part for Anand's absence, and things seem to grow bright. The tone of his last letter to Anand is one of joy and thanksgiving. His death is then reported flatly in the paper, and Shama's sisters visit for the cremation ceremony on the banks of a muddy stream, followed by the return of Shama and the children to the empty house.

COMMENTARY: Some points and details given in the Prologue are repeated here and expanded. The technique of reporting Mr Biswas's death in an impersonal form, as an item in a newspaper, adds to the pathos of his death and prevents any note of melodrama or sentimentality. The elegiac mood is also continued in the constraint and control of the final paragraph with its closing image of the empty house. This image also emphasises the significance of the house as a symbol in the novel.

Part 3

Commentary

The achievement of the novel

A House for Mr Biswas is a rich novel which presents a picture of life in Trinidad during a period of about fifty years; the development of the characters and the plot itself take place against a changing social background. The centre of the novel is always the character of Mr Biswas, and the themes are closely linked with him. Although he is an ordinary person with no outstanding features, Naipaul succeeds in giving him a heroic status and, as readers, we sympathise with his struggles, his failures and successes. He is in many ways an archetypal figure in that he embodies a universal theme – the search for identity and for meaning in life, and it is this search which is charted in the novel and provides much of its humour. We also see in the novel the rise and fall of the Tulsi family, and the cultural transitions which the different generations have to undergo. Mr Biswas himself is a man caught between two cultures and unable to settle fully in either. As a second-generation Indian, whose grandfather crossed the 'black waters' from India, he is part of the Indians' attempt to recreate their world in the predominantly Creole society of Trinidad. Naipaul shows this attempt as doomed to failure. In an informative essay on Trinidad in his travel book *The Middle Passage*, he describes vividly the Hindu world of the Tulsis as: 'an enclosing self-sufficient world absorbed with its quarrels and jealousies, as difficult for the outsider to penetrate as for one of its own members to escape. It protected and imprisoned, a static world, awaiting decay'.

Any study of the themes of the novel is best approached through a close study of the character of Mr Biswas, and the themes can be defined during this examination.

The character of Mr Biswas

Mohun Biswas (who is referred to as Mr Biswas even when still a small baby) is a person who is subject to misfortune, as the ill omens present at his birth suggest. He is marked, however, by his continual resilience and optimism. Despite his feeling of being trapped by the Tulsis, he fights to maintain his independence and feels confident that life will eventually yield to him its sweetness and romance. A sense of despair and disillusionment troubles him later in life, but he fights against that too, and retains faith in the future both through his children and through achieving the status of a house-owner. At Hanuman House he conducts his campaign against the Tulsis with humour and inventiveness which show his wit and sense of absurdity. He invents a catalogue of animal names for the family, such as 'the old hen' for Mrs Tulsi, and mocks them for their strong and exclusive family loyalties and mixed religious affinities. At times his actions can seem petty and spiteful, and yet Naipaul succeeds in retaining our respect and liking for him as a character. It is worth thinking about how Naipaul achieves this difficult balance. Part of the answer is that Mr Biswas is able to make fun of himself as well as of other people, and so avoids becoming too superior and smug. He acts the role of clown or buffoon frequently, and even mocks his own appearance. In a scene at The Chase, he reflects how he does not feel like a small man, and yet the clothes hanging up were unmistakably those of 'a small man, comic, make-believe clothes'. A sense of insecurity also remains with him, so that he never feels periods of good fortune can be permanent, or believes in them fully. The effort to achieve the ownership of his house, reflected in the very title of the novel, thus becomes a need to establish a firm reality and independence of his own. The creativity shown in his painting and writing reflects this need further, as does his reading of fiction and philosophy. He needs to believe in the possibility of romance, and much of his frustration in the novel stems from the feeling that romance is always eluding him, especially after he becomes involved with the Tulsis.

This involvement reveals another major theme of the novel: that of the complex relationship between freedom and commitment. Freedom is shown as something which is desired, but feared at the same time, as it can cause feelings of emptiness and of not belonging or being necessary to another person or to society as a whole. These feelings are frequently at war in Mr Biswas, and this conflict is shown in his changing attitudes to Hanuman House. Although he quickly rebels against its attempt to destroy his individuality by making him conform to the established rules and codes of behaviour, he also welcomes the feeling of security and orderliness which it offers. Here he is no longer simply a nonentity, but has a recognised role, even if it often seems a negative one. He himself feels on occasions that his campaign is pointless and degrading, and that his presence in the household is basically irrelevant since if he left, the family rituals would continue as before.

It is at this point, at the end of Part 1, that he recognises that rebellion – to be constructive – must be accompanied by the positive act of constructing a better alternative, and he leaves for the city with this intention. The process of building a separate identity and accepting the results of one's past actions and involvements is shown to be a painful and difficult process. It involves the shedding of fantasies and illusions we all possess, symbolised for Mr Biswas in his 'Escape' stories which he eventually destroys, and accepting the reality and commitments which have (like Mr Biswas's possessions) gradually accumulated almost without his being aware of it. The novel is thus partly about growing up, and attaining maturity and a sense of responsibility.

A similar ambivalence is shown in Mr Biswas's religious views. Although he claims to reject any traditional Hindu attitudes, such as the rigid caste system (as is shown when he joins the Aryans), he enjoys his Brahmin status when at Tara's and Ramchand's homes, and possesses a certain fastidiousness about foods and smells – he refuses to stock salt beef and lard in his shop at The Chase, and in moments of fear and stress he chants Hindu phrases. He also receives a traditional Hindu cremation. Naipaul is showing us here the complex relationship that exists between the forces that shape an individual and his attempts to form his own personality and beliefs.

Mr Biswas displays also a certain naïvety or innocence in the judgements he forms of other people. It seems that he can be easily misled by people who can take advantage of his fears and ambitions. This deception happens with Moti and the lawyer Seebaran at The Chase; with the carpenter, Maclean, at Green Vale; and with the solicitor's clerk. At Hanuman House also he is deceived into thinking that he is marrying into a wealthy family and will receive a large dowry, but this hope proves hollow. A further concept that Naipaul is illustrating in the novel is the difference that can exist between appearance and reality, and this contrast is often a source of humour. The walls of Hanuman House appear to be concrete, but are in fact, as Mrs Tulsi proudly tells him, made of clay bricks. This disparity is shown most clearly in the house in Sikkim Street which again looks deceptively solid and deceives Mr Biswas, and then, comically, the Tuttles.

Mr Biswas himself is not all that he appears to be. As he says sadly to Shama: 'That is the whole blasted trouble. I don't look like anything at all. Shopkeeper, lawyer, doctor, labourer, overseer – I don't look like any of them.' As one of the Tulsi sons-in-law and as a journalist he can achieve a kind of status, but has always to return to his 'crowded, shabby room'. During his job as investigator of Deserving Destitutes, he reflects that the conditions he is living in are as bad as the people about whom he is writing. This element of vulnerability and lack of certainty help to make Mr Biswas into a human and sympathetic person, as well as a kind of Everyman with whom we can identify. This also explains his words to his son during his breakdown at Green Vale when Anand asks him in a bewildered way 'Who are you?' Mr Biswas replies: 'I am just somebody. Nobody at all. I am just a man you know'. Thus he resents, as we all do, the attempts of other people to categorise him and so reduce his individuality. He even alters his daughter's birth certificate where he is described by Seth as a labourer, and signs himself 'proprietor'.

His attempts at self-definition, then, constitute the main body of the novel. By finally owning his own house away from the Tulsis, who are described at the end of the prologue as 'that large, disintegrating and indifferent family', he has succeeded in laying claim to his portion of the earth and escaped the fate of having 'lived and died as one had been born, unnecessary and unaccommodated'.

Mr Biswas and the other main characters

To understand and appreciate Mr Biswas fully, it is necessary to examine his relationship with three characters who are of particular importance to him: his son, his mother and his wife. His relationship with his son is close and often tense as they recognise in each other a common weakness and vulnerability. Each feels responsible for the other, and one senses that Anand, in particular, sometimes resents this emotional tie. This point may explain why, at the end of the novel, he decides not to return home when his father is dying. It is also significant that it was during this period, after Mr Biswas was sacked from the *Sentinel*, that he most needed 'his son's interest and anger' since 'in all the world there was no one else to whom he could complain'. Mr Biswas seems much closer to his son than he is to his wife Shama, as they share many characteristics and Anand models himself on his father. When Mr Biswas first starts to take an interest in his son, after initially regarding him as a disappointment, he is struck by the fragility of his appearance. Their first real contact occurs when Anand chooses to remain with his father at Green Vale because, as he shyly admits, 'they was going to leave you alone'. Another link between them is established here – that of education, as Mr Biswas teaches his son about Copernicus, and later introduces him to Dickens and other novelists. He is anxious that his son should not be like him; he wants him to succeed in a worthwhile career, and his hopes for the future increasingly focus on his son. He pays for private lessons and the esteemed diet of milk and prunes, and even helps with the writing of his essays. Despite Anand's claim that he does not want to be like his father when he is older, the boy is strongly influenced by him, and also in a sense learns from his mistakes and difficulties. Thus we are told that, among the children at Shorthills, Anand is considered strong, though he is kept apart because of his 'satirical sense'. This began at first as 'only a pose, and imitation of his father' but then developed into an attitude of contempt which led to 'inadequacies . . . self-awareness and a lasting loneliness' and also made him 'unassailable'. Though Mr Biswas uses his gifts of caricature and humour to protect himself, particularly at Hanuman House, we still feel his essential vulnerability and suffering, partly because of his strong need and desire to belong and feel at home in society. Unlike his son, he can never sustain an attitude of detachment and aloofness for any length of time.

The relationship between Mr Biswas and his mother, though it is not dealt with at any length, is felt as a strong force in the novel, and is treated by Naipaul with great delicacy and sensitivity. The relationship is expressed largely in negative terms in its effect on Mr Biswas. After the death of his father, Mr Biswas looks to his mother for greater support and comfort. After he returns from the rum shop, he asks his mother sadly why she keeps sending him to live with other people, and complains that: 'I have no father to look after me and people can treat me how they want'. When they live together at the back trace in Pagotes, she fills him with anger and depression as she constantly bewails her fate, and is shy of showing him affection in a house of strangers. He turns to Tara for motherly support – it is to her that he recounts the humiliating tale of the bananas, in the hope of being comforted.

There is, however, a shift in Mr Biswas's view of his mother in the novel. He realises that she is a woman who is still energetic and capable when he visits her at Pagotes during his period at The Chase, and again when he sees her at Pratap's home during his travels as the Scarlet Pimpernel. She comes to stay with him at Shorthills for a fortnight and again surprises Mr Biswas and wins his respect by her efficiency, and by the calmness and acceptance with which she views their relationship. He still, however, feels very guilty about his mother, knowing that he has neglected her in the past and has felt ashamed of her poverty. He feels after her death that he has never known her or loved her, and his poetic tribute to her – as well as his lengthy letter to the doctor – are attempts to express his grief and guilt, and so come to terms with them and be 'whole' again. This guilt also influences Mr Biswas's purchase of the house in Sikkim Street when the solicitor's clerk uses the pretext of needing to provide his own ageing mother with greater comfort as the reason for a quick sale. Naipaul succeeds in presenting this flawed relationship, linked as it is with a sense of loss and of 'something missed', without any traces of sentimentality or idealisation. This is one of his great strengths as a novelist: in his treatment of Mr Biswas and other characters, he is able to blend a certain detachment and objectivity with human warmth and compassion.

The same comment can be made about the relationship between Mr Biswas and his wife. This, too, is flawed in that neither husband nor wife really understands each other. Shama, with her mixed allegiances to the Tulsis and to her husband, remains largely a puzzle to her husband. Though she occasionally rebels against her husband for his disruptive behaviour, usually by leaving him, she is staunchly loyal and accepts what fate has given her. She is able to share his jokes about her family, though reminding him of his dependence on them. She fears any severing of her ties with the Tulsis since, as Mr Biswas recognises with an element of bitterness, ambition for her consists largely of 'a series of negatives: not to be unmarried, not to be childless, not to be an undutiful daughter, sister, wife, mother, widow'. Unlike her husband, she is happy to conform, and cannot understand the necessity for his rebellion.

Nonetheless Mr Biswas is glad of her presence and company. At The Chase, for example, she banishes the silence and loneliness, and his breakdown at Green Vale is partly caused by her long absences with the children and his subsequent isolation. He comes increasingly to rely on her powers of judgement, even though he still acts independently, as over the purchase of his last house. He is sometimes embarrassed by her lack of education, as in the scene with Miss Logie, where Shama talks garrulously to her during the drive to Sans-Souci. This scene also shows that Mr Biswas is unaware of certain aspects of his wife's character, just as he was surprised to find her childhood mementoes, signs of her contact with the outside world, in the drawer of the dressing-table during their move to Green Vale. In spite of its inadequacies, the marriage tie is shown as strong and enduring, providing a point around which both characters can build and define their lives.

Style and structure

The novel is divided into two parts, enclosed by a Prologue and an Epilogue. The plot structure is part of a long British novelistic tradition as represented by Charles Dickens (1812–70) with its concentration on the life history of a single protagonist, and the tracing of his fortunes from birth to death, with the accompanying search for self-fulfilment and recognition. The novel also traces the rise and fall of the Tulsi family, and the changes in society over a period of fifty years. It is difficult to date the events in the novel precisely, but it seems to cover the period between 1905 and 1951, so including the two major world wars – the second of which does impinge on the novel with its economic effects and the growing American influence. Naipaul, however, does not wholly conform to the model defined above. The hero's death, for instance, is reported in the Prologue, and throughout the novel there is a subtle series of cross-references and recurring images. A minor example of the latter is the description of the legs of Pratap and Prasad on returning from the muddy buffalo pond which had turned white 'so that they looked like the trees in fire-stations and police-stations which are washed with white lime up to the middle of their trunks', an image which Mr Biswas recalls when he leaves Hanuman House and Arwacas after his period of convalescence and sees the palm trees in the drive to the police-station. A more notable example is the catalogue of Mr Biswas's possessions which is used to represent different phases of his life and to act as a concrete reference to his past experiences. At each move to another house, the growing list is detailed. After the time at Shorthills, for example, Mr Biswas has gained 'only two pieces of furniture: the Slumberking bed and Théophile's bookcase'. For the reader, also, each item of furniture becomes overlaid with particular associations, and so helps to bind the novel together and give it unity. A feeling of pathos is also evoked by the list of these 'gatherings of a lifetime' when they are exposed for the last time on the move to Sikkim Street and seem 'unfamiliar and shabby and shameful'.

Perhaps the most striking characteristic of Naipaul's style is his power of observation. He shows precision and clarity, as well as a close attention to detail and an ability to create mood and atmosphere in a realistic and evocative way. He comments in *An Area of Darkness* that landscapes are not truly real until they have been given the quality of myth; but there is always a solidity and concreteness about his descriptions. The barracks at Green Vale, for example, are described at one point as 'a place that was nowhere, a dot on the map of the island, which was a dot on the map of the world'. This abstract comment is then followed by the observation that ' . . . dead trees ringed the barracks, a wall of flawless black'. Naipaul does not flinch from describing unpleasant sights, such as the scabs formed by the sores which Mr Biswas has as a child, but the language used is never sensational or exaggerated. This sense of control comes partly from the distance that Naipaul maintains from the material he is handling, which enables him to avoid falsely romanticising his subject and makes the material seem realistic and credible. An example of this is the careful detailing of Mr Biswas's breakdown at Green Vale. By reporting this process in an unemotional tone, usually in the form of statements, he gives the writing great power and dramatic effect. When Mr Biswas moves into his incomplete house, he becomes obsessed with the asphalt on the roof which melts and looks like a number of snakes. They even begin to appear in his dreams, and 'He began to regard them as living, and wondered what it would be like to have one fall and curl on his skin'. When this horror occurs, it is reported in a matter-of-fact way which serves to intensify the horror far more than a more melodramatic description could have done. 'A snake had fallen on him. Very thin, and not long. When they looked up they saw the parent snake, waiting to release some more'.

This restraint in the writing is a difficult achievement for any writer, and is one of Naipaul's great strengths. We experience the sufferings of Mr Biswas more intensely because of this careful and delicate contrast between the awfulness of a particular event and the contained way in which it is described. A further example is the destruction of the doll's house which Mr Biswas has given his daughter, one of the most traumatic experiences which he has in the novel. Once again, however, the event is described in a simple style which allows the reader to imagine the emotions involved vividly. Mr Biswas discovers the doll's house thrown against a fence in the yard at Hanuman House: 'A broken door, a ruined window, a staved-in wall or even roof – he had expected that. But not this. The doll's house did not exist. He saw only a bundle of firewood. None of its parts was whole. Its delicate joints were exposed and useless'.

Symbolism and imagery

The example of the doll's house also shows the powerful use of symbolism in the novel. Here the doll's house, and its destruction, are identified with Mr Biswas himself. The house appears to have a human body, with the references to 'delicate joints' and later to 'torn skin'. There are many uses of symbolism in the novel: symbols can be linked with places and with people, or with both. Thus the description of Hanuman House as an 'alien white fortress' suggests the foreign nature of the Tulsis and their Hindu religion in Trinidad, and the way in which the house will be a prison to Mr Biswas against which he must rebel with his own weapons. This could be termed a 'multiple' symbol since it evokes more than one image, and there are several other symbols which operate in this way. There is the recurrent image of the boy standing outside a house at dusk which Mr Biswas first observes when acting as a conductor on one of Ajodha's buses. It becomes associated for him with a feeling of desolation and loneliness, and is linked symbolically with his need for stability and a home to give a sense of certainty and security. Naipaul also uses descriptions of nature and landscape to echo the themes of the novel and to act as symbols. When associated with the Tulsis, the landscape often takes the form of an uncontrolled and decaying jungle. The shop at The Chase is surrounded by abandoned land which fosters nettles and weeds, and around Green Vale there are half-dead leaves, and it is 'damp and shadowed and close'. At Shorthills the fertile and productive land is largely uncultivated and becomes a wilderness. In Mr Biswas's house in Sikkim Street, however, nature is seen as something beautiful and even lyrical, with the coolness of the laburnum and the scent of the lily which comfort Mr Biswas during his final illness. When he plants a garden at Mrs Tulsi's house in Port of Spain the rose trees flourish; but as his despair and disillusionment deepen, the roses, untended, grow 'straggly and hard' and are damaged by a blight. The symbolism in the novel is rarely obtrusive or heavy-handed, and, like the central symbol of the house itself, the symbols gradually accumulate additional force and meaning in the course of the novel.

One isolated symbol which deserves comment is the image of the winged ants which Anand watches during the storm at Green Vale. In this episode we see the destruction of one type of ant by another more fitted to survive. Anand tries to kill the black, biting ants but abandons this as futile when he is suddenly terrified by their anger and vindictiveness. This episode can be seen as illustrating the compassion that Anand feels for the victim, but also his frustration and anger when he recognises the futility of the weak trying to help the weak. These feelings are echoed in his relationship with his father, particularly at this moment when Mr Biswas is huddled on the bed reciting Hindu words, and imagining that 'they' have come to get him.

Humour and satire

These two elements are central in the novel and are often linked, since satire uses ridicule, irony, and sarcasm to criticise its object. Irony is the dominant technique for creating humour, particularly in the descriptions of the feuds between Mr Biswas and the Tulsis. Mr Biswas comments to Shama at one point, when she is threatening to return to Hanuman House after a quarrel, that she will be given 'some medal at the monkey house'; and he invents animal names for the main members of the family, as well as referring to Mrs Tulsi's two sons as the 'little gods'. These descriptions, though absurd and farcical, also contain some truth and so gain our sympathy and we laugh with Mr Biswas at the pretensions and petty tyrannies of the Tulsis. Particular incidents at the Tulsi establishment are also humorous and even border on slapstick, such as the spilling of a plate of food on Owad's head. The humour is also directed at times against Mr Biswas himself; this adds to the complexity and richness of the novel since it avoids a simplified response in the reader, and also contributes to the picture we have of Mr Biswas's character. Thus, when he refers to Hanuman House as being like a 'blasted zoo', Shama comments that he has the role of a barking puppy dog, a description which, again, contains an element of truth. Mr Biswas is frequently satirised in the novel, and his weaknesses exposed. The use of the third person – Mr Biswas – creates in itself a distancing effect for the reader, and we see Mr Biswas as essentially a complex and rounded character. There is humour in his battle for possessions with W. C. Tuttle at the house in Port of Spain, a battle in which he is fully engaged and which continues until he finally buys his own house. A similar rivalry is shown with Govind over clothes. There is a humorous scene when Mr Biswas dresses up in his expensive new suit and goes to a cricket match to show it off, only to find that the match is almost over.

There are many other instances of humour in the novel. Owad's superficial conversion to the Russian Revolution is held up to ridicule, and Anand's speedy rejection of his hero's stated artistic prejudices is treated similarly, though with more sympathy. There is often, however, a contrasting sense of pathos and even desperation underlying the humour. Mr Biswas himself suggests this in his response to his quarrels with the Tulsis. These quarrels, as with the final one which causes him to leave Mrs Tulsi's house, often leave him with a feeling of humiliation and indignity: 'Mr Biswas's anger had gone stale; it burdened him. Now there was also shame at his behaviour, shame at the whole gross scene'. A similar point is made by the story of Billy which is recounted gleefully in the café where Mr Biswas has gone with the solicitor's clerk. It is a tale about people being cheated out of houses and it causes laughter ' . . . but Mr Biswas could take no part in it'. There is undiluted humour in the novel, but frequently a more sombre note is present and undercuts the comedy.

Tragedy or comedy?

A House for Mr Biswas cannot be fitted neatly into a specific critical category or genre. It has elements of the comic and the tragic, and often the distinctions are blurred. We see Mr Biswas undergoing much suffering and frustration but often retaliating in a comic manner with his gestures of rebellion. He sees himself in a rather wry and sardonic manner; comparing himself with Hari in their respective positions in the Tulsi hierarchy, he reflects that ' . . . he couldn't see himself as a holy man for long. Sooner or later someone was bound to surprise him . . . reading "The Manxman" or "The Atom"', and, although he may sometimes resent acting the role of a clown or buffoon, his inherent wit and facetiousness make this role inevitable. His small physique and continual indigestion are also sources of humour. He has much in common with Willy Loman in the play *Death of a Salesman* (1949) by Arthur Miller (*b*.1915); both have elements of the tragic hero. Like the traditional tragic hero, Mr Biswas suffers and dies, and still retains his ideals and vision in the face of opposition, showing great resilience in the process. Though he may seem absurd and self-deluded at times, as in his final purchase of a house, our response to him is mixed, and we can admire his endurance and sympathise with his vulnerability. There is also at the end of the novel a sense of resolution and of something achieved which is more appropriate to comedy than tragedy, where the predominant feeling at the end is often a sense of waste. Mr Biswas dies with the comforting knowledge that he is not, like King Lear in Shakespeare's tragedy, 'unnecessary and unaccommodated', but has left a legacy to his wife and children in the triumphant acquisition of a house.

The minor characters

Mrs Tulsi

Mrs Tulsi is the centre of the Tulsi family around which the other characters revolve. She is the widow of Pundit Tulsi, a respected figure both in his native India and in Trinidad, and the whole family gain prestige from his reputation. Mrs Tulsi (or 'Mai', meaning mother, as she is frequently called) maintains a matriarchal tyranny over the household and its various members. It is significant that in Hanuman House, the usual Hindu tradition by which daughters go to live with their husbands and become almost servants of their mothers-in-law is reversed, in that the husbands stay in the daughters' household and become subservient to their mother-in-law, Mrs Tulsi. This is part of the humiliation which Mr Biswas feels so strongly and tries to reject. The manipulation which Mrs Tulsi directs towards those around her is cleverly concealed (though not from Mr Biswas) under an appearance of martyrdom and suffering. If someone steps out of line, she faints and retires to the Rose Room where she is endlessly massaged by the faithful Sushila and other daughters, and remains there until the offending son-in-law, who encounters silence and hostility on all sides, is forced to capitulate and apologise to her.

Mr Biswas is on many occasions subject to the whims and emotional blackmail of the 'old fox'. She is able to control her moods according to the occasion, to become maudlin and sentimental to disarm her opponent. This is shown when she tries to win Mr Biswas back to family allegiance after the birth of Savi, whom he wishes to name Lakshmi. She makes a number of simple statements which strike Mr Biswas as possessing a 'puzzling profundity', and he finds himself listening against his will and being 'trapped' by her mood. She is proud of her authority and her 'old-fashionedness', and the floggings she has administered to her daughters have become legendary. She will also resort to a biting sarcasm when necessary and Mr Biswas, on first meeting her, is struck by her command of English. When Mr Biswas offends against the Tulsi demand for the suppression of individuality by buying the large doll's house for Savi, Mrs Tulsi declares that she is poor and gives to all but cannot 'compete with Santa Claus' and she asks Shama to give her notice before moving to 'her mansion'. Like her brother-in-law Seth, who rules with her, she is capable of surprising crudity in her language as when she tells Mr Biswas to 'go to hell' during their final quarrel.

The novel shows the decline of the Tulsi family which is caused by internal wrangles and the disruptive effects of a different culture. Mrs Tulsi is anxious for her sons to succeed and sends them to a Roman Catholic college, thus compromising her Hindu beliefs – as Mr Biswas is quick to point out with his image of her as 'the orthodox Roman Catholic Hindu' who has salmon only on Good Friday. Mrs Tulsi moves to Port of Spain when she feels that the 'younger god' Owad should be looked after during his schooling following his brother's marriage. It is at this point that the power structure in Hanuman House begins to be threatened, since Seth, though he can maintain control, fails to impose harmony. The family feud with Seth furthers the decline of the household, and when Owad is sent abroad to study to become a doctor, Mrs Tulsi appears to lose interest in the family and ceases to direct it until she is revived by the move to Shorthills. Here again, however, her interest soon languishes, though she issues some directives about food and possible economies. We are told that, after the death of Mrs Tulsi's sister, Padma, the 'virtue' of the family dissolves, and Mrs Tulsi assumes more and more the role of an invalid. She is still able to exert control over her daughters, and on her move to the city from Shorthills, succeeds in making their lives a misery as she develops her command 'of invective and obscenity'. She is revived by the return of Owad, and exerts herself to please him while her health improves 'spectacularly' under his treatment, thus betraying her obvious hypochondria. After Owad is alienated by the quarrel with Anand and his increasing association with his own friends and Dorothy's cousin, she tries in vain to win him back by talking about his boyhood and Pundit Tulsi and her own sufferings; but it is now too late. She is a character for whom the reader feels little sympathy, but she is a source of much humour and satire in the novel, as well as showing the decline of traditions through her failure to maintain them. We also see, through her involvement with Roman Catholicism, the dilution of Hindu culture and religious ritual.

Seth

Seth, the husband of Padma, is presented as a powerful figure in the novel who intimidates Mr Biswas with his bullying manner and the self-assured way in which he flourishes his ivory cigarette holder though dressed in muddy boots and a stained khaki topee. He shows contempt for those who are not prepared to work on the land and dirty their hands, and is nicknamed the 'big thug' by Mr Biswas. He is a staunch supporter of family loyalty in the first half of the novel and conducts the family tribunals, where the misdemeanours of Mr Biswas are criticised and ridiculed. It is Seth who names him 'the paddler' and who refers to the house being turned into a republic with a 'serpent' in its midst. Seth is still shown as possessing some good points; at times he shows a brusque kindness to Mr Biswas – addressing him as Mohun, joking with him over the birth of his first child, and rescuing him from trouble with the police when cycling without a light, though this is partly to protect the family name. There is a note of amused irony in some of his comments to Mr Biswas which suggests that he is both puzzled and amused by his persistent rebellion. Thus he questions him about his 'dear friend', Pankaj Rai, and jokes that he will now have 'Creole converts' as brothers. In contrast to the rather naïve Mr Biswas, Seth appears a worldly figure with his plans to 'insuranburn' and his later business ventures, and he seems to adopt an avuncular attitude to the former at times. After his breakdown at Green Vale, Seth says 'I suppose we have to bring the paddler home'.

It is Seth's disaffection, which begins obscurely with an internal family quarrel involving Shekhar, that marks the break-up of the close family network. Seth begins to be seen as an outsider, and his character is adversely affected. We see this when he comes to uproot the rose bushes in Mrs Tulsi's garden to make room for his lorries. He tells Mr Biswas's children that everyone seems to be defying him, and rather cruelly tells them that their father was 'picked up' by him when 'catching flies'. He is excluded from the move to Shorthills as the disagreement becomes open war, and starts to claim Tulsi property as his own, even attempting to establish a rival store. The feud then dwindles after he gets involved in legal charges against him, and becomes 'quiescent'. Our last view of him is of a rather sad and pathetic figure, dressed incongruously in a cheap suit, trying in vain to effect a reconciliation with the family through Owad on the latter's return. Like Mr Biswas, we feel sympathy for Seth here, with the contrast between his present position and the one he occupied previously at Hanuman House.

Owad

Owad, the younger of the two 'little gods', is noted for his terrible temper as a boy, and he confronts Mr Biswas directly and wants him to apologise to his mother for calling her names. He accuses Mr Biswas of being a Christian after he rejects the offering at the morning *puja*. He is also the victim of the contents of the plateful of food which Mr Biswas throws from the balcony, and urges Govind to kill Mr Biswas during their tussle. This conflict is later forgotten when Owad and Mr Biswas form a friendship while living at the house in Port of Spain, based on a mutual respect for each other's intellectual pursuits, and Mr Biswas is upset and envious when Owad goes abroad. On the latter's return, there is a distance between them, and Owad becomes largely a comic figure whom Naipaul satirises for boasting about his contacts and importance abroad and for his superficial and short-lived adherence to the Russian Revolution. Being viewed as the new head of the family, he is listened to and consulted as an absolute authority. We learn that because of Owad's objections to the behaviour and habits of Indians from India, who were 'a disgrace' to Trinidad Indians, in one afternoon 'the family reverence for India had been shattered'. He emphasises physical strength and manual skills, and entertains the family by recounting his adventures. His allegiances soon shift to his own friends, the 'new caste' of educated professional men, and his friendship with Dorothy, the renegade Presbyterian sister-in-law, leads to his eventual marriage to Dorothy's Presbyterian cousin, an Indian girl from South Trinidad. In this way, he reflects the changes that have taken place in the society at this period.

Shekhar

Shekhar is the other 'little god'. He figures little in the earlier part of the novel, and, after initial rebelliousness, marries a Presbyterian girl whose family have successful commercial concerns. He leaves Hanuman

House and goes to live with his wife's family, thus going against the Hindu custom and the family tradition of bringing the bride home. He prospers as a businessman, though reputedly envying his brother his travel abroad, having himself wanted to go to Cambridge. Like Owad, he becomes distant from the Tulsis and their traditions as he acquires more sophistication, shown by his parting gifts to his brother: a bottle of wine, American magazines, and an English history book. He also runs cinemas as part of his business, and offends the widows by offering them work there, an insult which they regard as the influence of his wife, Dorothy. She displays Western influences: she wears short skirts, calls herself Dorothy, and 'flaunts' her education. She also speaks Spanish to her five daughters and her husband in the presence of her sisters-in-law. Both she and Shekhar are friendly with Mr Biswas, and later with Owad, though Mr Biswas comes to resent the role of buffoon to which they expect him to conform, and feels nervous and vulnerable when the party of Southern businessmen with whom Shekhar is involved issue veiled threats about the viability of the Community Welfare Department. But Shekhar's party is defeated in the colony's first general election, and Shekhar withdraws from public life to concentrate on his cinemas. Thus, like Owad, he reflects the decline of Hindu influences and the emphasis in the 'new' world on education and self-advancement.

Govind

Govind, whose wife Chinta is Shama's closest sister, is used as a contrast to Mr Biswas, particularly as regards their status and attitudes at Hanuman House. Mr Biswas is struck by the way Govind conforms to the Tulsi tyranny and is degraded in the process. In the presence of Seth, he becomes obsequious and weak in his anxiety to please. Mr Biswas is pained by the capitulation of this tall and handsome man and tries to spur him to rebellion. However, his abuse of the family is reported by Govind who is intent on protecting the family, as he shows again when he fights Mr Biswas for having insulted Owad. Their next contact is when Govind carries Mr Biswas into Hanuman House after he is brought from Green Vale, so putting himself 'on the side of authority'. He clearly finds security in Hanuman House which raises him from his former position as an illiterate coconut-seller.

After leaving Hanuman House, Govind attempts to become more independent. At Shorthills he sells trees from the estate, and becomes increasingly surly and bad-tempered. He buys a second-hand car and runs it as a taxi in Port of Spain. On the move to the city, he expands his business and acquires several suits which become part of the battle of possessions in the household. His rivalry with Mr Biswas is continued through their sons, Vidiadhar and Anand, who both study for the exhibition to the college. Govind then becomes increasingly violent and behaves in an odd and unpredictable manner, and is regarded as 'the terror of the house' until he takes to beating his wife and confines his aggression to that outlet.

Hari

Hari is another brother-in-law whose position at Hanuman House contrasts with that of Mr Biswas. He has won for himself a definite place of respect in the Tulsi hierarchy and is even excused from labouring work because of his reputation as a holy man and pundit, as well as his illnesses. He is a colourless man who ' . . . offended no one and amused no one', though Mr Biswas makes fun of him as the 'constipated holy man'. He takes no part in disputes and his apparent goodness is attributed largely to 'a negativeness that amounts to charity'. After his death, which evokes some pathos when we learn through Anand that he had known he was going to die for some time, he is found to have been indispensable. He is indirectly responsible for Mrs Tulsi's growing conversion to Roman Catholicism since she cannot find an adequate replacement for Hari at the *puja*. Like Govind, he suggests the price of conformity through the drabness of his character, and though Mr Biswas occasionally envies him his position in the Tulsi household, he knows that he himself could not live the life of a 'sick scholar'.

W. C. Tuttle

W. C. Tuttle functions mainly as a comic figure in the novel. He is named by Mr Biswas when he first meets him at Shorthills and they develop a rivalry over possessions, referring to each other's books as 'trash'. He is a man with a variety of interests and allegiances. He is a strict Hindu, proud of his Brahminical status, but is as interested in the material as the spiritual life. At Shorthills he engages in a number of business ventures, which include starting a furniture factory and a quarry. On the move to the city, he takes over most of Mrs Tulsi's house, and dominates the house with popular Western songs on his gramophone. He is 'all for modernity' and shocks the household by acquiring a statue of a naked woman. He regards himself as blending the Brahmin culture with the 'finer products' of Western civilisation, and views the Tulsis as barbarians, adopting towards most people an attitude of silent contempt which he conveys by a quivering of his nostrils. He appears to win decisively the battle of possessions when he acquires his own house, a move to which Mr Biswas reacts 'badly', but the latter is compensated when the Tuttles come to visit him at his own house in Sikkim Street and are clearly impressed by the house, even being somewhat jealous of its apparent size and comfort.

Ajodha

Ajodha is the husband of Tara, and uncle to Mr Biswas. He is a man of wealth who has freed himself from the land, and was one of the first men in Trinidad to buy a car. The chief fascination he has for Mr Biswas during the latter's childhood is when he asks Mr Biswas to read him the newspaper column entitled 'That Body of Yours', a job which is later taken over by Anand. He functions later as a model of contentment for Mr Biswas, since he possesses his own house and has an attentive wife. To the Tulsis, however, he is a renegade who has deserted the Hindu faith and aligned himself with wealth, comfort and modernity. He becomes increasingly preoccupied with his quarrels with his two nephews, Jagdat and Rabidat, who live with him after being deserted by their own father. He feels bound to his nephews since, like Mrs Tulsi, he fears being alone in his old age, and distrusts strangers too much to allow them to help in his business. The model of family contentment thus becomes an illusion on Mr Biswas's part, as he recognises himself. It is significant that he goes to Ajodha to borrow the money for his house and thus reinforces his ties to his own family, rather than depending on the Tulsis as before.

Tara

Tara is Bipti's more powerful sister. She is regarded as a person of standing through her marriage to the wealthy Ajodha. When Raghu dies, she takes over the funeral arrangements in an energetic and capable manner, and is scornful of her sister's ignorance of her husband's financial affairs. She adopts a motherly role towards Mr Biswas and she decides to have him trained as a pundit. It is she to whom he returns later with his children on a series of regular visits, from which his wife excludes herself because of the old antagonism between the two families. Tara also has strong moral standards; she refuses to allow Dehuti to be mentioned after she elopes with Tara's yard boy, Ramchand, thus depriving her of two family servants, and her brother-in-law Bhandat receives the same treatment because of his drunkenness and Chinese mistress.

Bhandat

Bhandat, the brother of Ajodha, is a symbol of failure and destitution. He is a small man with a whining voice and irritable manner. He drinks and cheats by altering the accounts in the rum shop which he runs for his brother, helped briefly by Mr Biswas. He reappears later as a destitute in the city, and writes to Mr Biswas for help. When the latter visits him, he adopts a sentimental and self-pitying manner, as well as playing the schoolboy prank of pulling Mr Biswas's hair. He is clearly frustrated and tormented and abuses his Chinese mistress in Hindi. He himself is deaf, and is a figure for whom we feel a mixture of contempt and pity in his futile attempts to compose slogans for a competition, and the squalor in which he lives.

Part 4

Hints for study

A House for Mr Biswas is a long and detailed novel and so needs close and repeated study. It is useful, as you read the novel, to keep a pen in your hand to underline those passages which illustrate particular points about character and themes, which you can then transfer on to separate sheets of notes for the purpose of essay-writing and revision for the examination. It is essential that you should be able to illustrate your argument about a character or an idea with relevant and carefully chosen quotations. Always read the question carefully; it will normally be about one of the following:

(*a*)   themes
(*b*)   characters and their relationships
(*c*)   particular passages, and how they relate to the rest of the work.

In all cases the student should pay careful attention to the construction of his essay, and it is useful to make some notes before you begin writing about the main points you will need to cover. By doing this you should avoid omitting a vital point. Your essay should be presented in an orderly way, as the following model suggests:

(*a*)   opening paragraph discussing the meaning and implications of the question and possible ways of treating it
(*b*)   development of your argument with relevant detailed reference to the text
(*c*)   conclusion – a paragraph in which you summarise the main points of your argument briefly, referring back to the question asked.

There are also common faults which the student should try to avoid when answering a question:

(*a*)   re-telling the plot; material chosen must relate directly to the question asked, and no question will ever demand a simple account of the story
(*b*)   treating a question about theme as a character-study; these two elements of the novel may be linked but are still separate and distinct

(c) misunderstanding or evading the question; questions should be read very carefully, since careless reading often leads students into irrelevant or distorted answers. Students should also avoid the writing out of a 'prepared' answer.

Specimen questions

(1) To what extent do you see Mr Biswas as a heroic figure?

(2) '*A House for Mr Biswas* is a novel about the relationship between father and son'. How far do you agree with this description?

(3) Is *A House for Mr Biswas* a suitable title for the novel?

(4) Analyse and discuss the conflicts within the Tulsi family.

(5) Show how the themes of rebellion and freedom form a major part of the novel.

(6) Examine the use of contrast in the novel by looking at any three of the following characters: (*i*) Hari (*ii*) Govind (*iii*) Bipti (*iv*) Mrs Tulsi (*v*) Seth.

(7) Trace the changes in society which take place in the course of the novel.

(8) Read the following passage carefully, and answer the questions below: 'He read innumerable novels, particularly those in the Reader's Library; and he even tried to write, encouraged by the appearance in a Port of Spain magazine of a puzzling story by Misir. (This was a story of a starving man who was rescued by a benefactor and after some years rose to wealth. One day, driving along the beach, the man heard someone in the sea shouting for help, and recognized his former benefactor in difficulties; he instantly dived into the water, struck his head on a submerged rock and was drowned. The benefactor survived.) But Mr Biswas could never devise a story, and he lacked Misir's tragic vision; whatever his mood and however painful his subject, he became irreverent and facetious as soon as he began to write, and all he could manage were distorted and scurrilous descriptions of Moti, Mungroo, Seebaran, Seth and Mrs Tulsi.' (p. 183)

(*i*) Relate the passage briefly to its context.

(*ii*) What does the passage contribute to the novel in terms of theme and character-portrayal?

Model answers

(2) '*A House for Mr Biswas* is a novel about the relationship between father and son'. How far do you agree with this description?

Anand is not born until a third of the way through the book; and it is not until he wakes one Christmas morning at Hanuman House with the momentary fear that there is no present for him, that he becomes a character with a mind of his own. Initially Mr Biswas feels that Anand belongs completely to the Tulsis and 'when he thought of his children... thought mainly of Savi'. The boy seems to him a disappointment with his frail and vulnerable appearance and the shy and tongue-tied manner which he possesses. Anand soon begins to assert himself, however, and the relationship with his father is one which grows in depth and understanding and which occupies a central position in the novel after the beginning of Mr Biswas's breakdown at Green Vale. Thus *A House for Mr Biswas* can be described as a novel about the father-son relationship, although it is concerned with other themes also, such as Mr Biswas's struggle for independence and his search for identity.

The relationship between father and son is intensified by the many traits they have in common. Mr Biswas shares his discovery of Dickens's novels with Anand and makes him write out and learn the meanings of difficult words. We are told that he does this not out of strictness or 'as part of Anand's training' but because he does not wish his son to be like him. His desires for his son centre on the idea that he should receive a good education and so be able to earn his living by following a profession which does not involve humiliation and dependence. He takes a close interest in his son's education, criticising his text-books, paying for private lessons, and for the diet of milk and prunes so valued by Mrs Tulsi. He even helps him to write an essay which he uses in the exhibition examination.

Anand seems to accept his father's interest and guidance, although resenting it at times as, for instance, when elaborate preparations are made for the examination and he has to take his father's wrist-watch and pen in case his own do not work. He understands his father's ambitions for him since, as Naipaul tells us in a revealing comment: 'Father and son, each saw the other as weak and vulnerable, and each felt a responsibility for the other, a responsibility which, in times of particular pain, was disguised by exaggerated authority on the one side, exaggerated respect on the other'. This protectiveness is perhaps the dominant note of their relationship. It is seen when Mr Biswas tells

Anand about his disgrace at Pundit Jairam's in order to comfort his son when he was in trouble for soiling his trousers at school; and again, on Anand's side, when he asserts that he will stay at Green Vale with his father because 'they was going to leave you alone'. He begins to take a close interest in his father; this is shown in a minor incident which again draws parallels between them. Anand objects to the rusty sheets of corrugated iron which Mr Biswas intends to use on his house at Green Vale but despite his objections Mr Biswas is firm in his decision to use it because it is cheap, and Anand says:

> 'All right go ahead and buy it and put it on your old house. I don't care what it look like now'.
> 'Another little paddler', Seth said.
> But Mr Biswas felt as Anand. He too didn't care what the house looked like now'.

Apart from the evidence here of shared feeling between father and son, Seth's comment on Anand is of interest since he does show traits of independence which arise partly from his 'satirical sense' which began as 'only a pose, and imitation of his father' but then developed into an attitude of contempt which led 'to inadequacies, to self-awareness and a lasting loneliness. But it made him unassailable.' This description refers to Anand as an adult rather than a child, and has an autobiographical element. Landeg White draws convincing parallels between Anand and Naipaul. He observes that 'Anand's discovery of his father is Naipaul's own discovery of Seepersad Naipaul'.* This element gives the novel another dimension and makes Naipaul's detachment and objectivity in describing this relationship all the more impressive.

The closeness between father and son is revealed in several episodes. A striking example occurs after Anand nearly drowns at the dockside where Mr Biswas was clowning with Owad and Shekhar and trying to get his son to join in. Anand is incensed and humiliated, and, as with his father's prose poem about his mother, uses writing to exorcise some of these emotions. The essay is dramatic and deeply felt and wins a high mark, though it does not conform to the teacher's plan. Mr Biswas reads it 'anxious to share the pain of the previous day'. He is anxious to be close to his son again to make up for 'the solitude of the previous day' when Anand had avoided him, and tells Anand to go through the essay with him. Anand refuses, and a row ensues until Anand retaliates by pulling his father's chair from under him at the dinner table, thus inflicting equal humiliation.

Anand is also concerned about his father's status, despite his claim

*V. S. Naipaul, a Critical Introduction, 1975, p. 94.

that he does not want to be like him. He is reassured when his father tells him that his schoolfriend's father is not his boss at the *Sentinel*, nor is he treated like an office boy. We see here the traditional idea of a son defining his identity against that of his father, but there is also the fear that his father is being badly treated. They are concerned about each other's successes and failures. When Anand is dejected after the examination, thinking he has failed, Mr Biswas tries to cheer him up by saying that 'No true effort is ever wasted', to which his son replies moodily 'What about you?' and though they sleep on the same bed 'neither spoke to the other for the rest of the evening'. Mr Biswas is then cheered by receiving a letter inviting him to join a literary group, and he repeats his adage about the value of true effort. Anand, however, recognises the extravagance of his father's elation 'but he was in no mood to give comfort, to associate himself with weakness' and 'he handed back the letter to Mr Biswas without a word'.

In the final section of the novel, where Mr Biswas is dismissed from the *Sentinel*, we are told that he 'needed his son's interest and anger' since 'In all the world there was no one else to whom he could complain'. Although he had earlier replied to his son's gloomy, self-pitying letters with long humorous ones, he now forgets Anand's own pain and sends him 'a hysterical, complaining, despairing letter' which elicits only a brief reply. Anand then goes back on his promise to return home, and is still in England when his father dies. This refusal to return can be interpreted as Anand's reluctance to associate himself with pain and weakness. A passage which occurs shortly before the Epilogue tells us, however, that Anand is not untouched by memories of his home and family. There is a detailed catalogue of memories which is seen through Anand's eyes and refers to 'a time of new separations and yearnings, in a library grown suddenly dark' when an association will trigger off thoughts of 'the hot noisy week before Christmas in the Tulsi Store'. This experience takes place in a 'northern land', presumably England, and Naipaul then concludes the passage: 'So later, and very slowly, in securer times of different stresses, when the memories had lost the power to hurt, with pain or joy, they would fall into place and give back the past'.

It is clear that *A House for Mr Biswas* is, to a large extent, a novel about the relationship between father and son, and the growing closeness and identification between them adds greatly to the richness and psychological realism of the novel.

(8) *Read the following passage carefully, and answer the questions below:*
'He read innumerable novels, particularly those in the Reader's Library; and he even tried to write, encouraged by the appearance in a Port of Spain magazine of a puzzling story by Misir. (This was a story of a starving man who was rescued by a benefactor and after some years rose to wealth. One day, driving along the beach, the man heard someone in the sea shouting for help, and recognized his former benefactor in difficulties; he instantly dived into the water, struck his head on a submerged rock and was drowned. The benefactor survived.) But Mr Biswas could never devise a story, and he lacked Misir's tragic vision; whatever his mood and however painful his subject, he became irreverent and facetious as soon as he began to write, and all he could manage were distorted and scurrilous descriptions of Moti, Mungroo, Seebaran, Seth and Mrs Tulsi'.
(*i*) Relate the passage briefly to its context.
(*ii*) What does the passage contribute to the novel in terms of theme and character-portrayal?

(*i*) The quoted passage occurs towards the end of Mr Biswas's stay at The Chase, when Naipaul is summarising the effect on Mr Biswas of the six years of 'boredom and futility' which he has experienced there. Shortly after this summary of his creative outlets, we learn that Shama has become pregnant for the third time and retires as usual to Hanuman House. Mr Biswas feels a change in his attitude to the Tulsi establishment as it comes to represent a refuge for him, a place of order where he has an accepted position and role. Although he is wary of Shama's efforts to persuade him to return there too, he eventually succumbs to her pressure and gladly leaves the dark and dusty shop. He is received back by the Tulsis and given work at Green Vale.

(*ii*) The passage centres on Mr Biswas's attempts to express himself creatively and so escape from the limitations of his environment and situation. He has tried painting also and has produced 'cool, ordered forest scenes' which are far removed from the rotting, mosquito-infested jungle which he can find within an hour's walk. The evident frustration he is feeling is thus expressed, and this is also shown by the shape his writing takes with the reference to 'distorted and scurrilous descriptions' of people who he feels have been against him.

Mungroo is a man from the village, the leader of the village stick-fighters, who owes credit at the shop, and Mr Biswas is persuaded by Moti to sue him for owing money, through the offices of the corrupt lawyer, Seebaran. Moti exploits Mr Biswas's fears of being taken advantage of, and of becoming bankrupt and destitute like the hero of one of Misir's stories. It emerges, however, that none of the credit notes which Mr Biswas possesses have been signed, since Mr Biswas thought it 'discourteous' to demand a signature. He has to pay Moti five dollars initially, which causes a quarrel with Shama and her return to the 'monkey house', and then finds himself charged for defaming Mungroo's reputation for which he had to pay a hundred dollars. This sum is borrowed from Misir, who, besides being a writer, has set himself up as a usurer with a capital of two hundred dollars. This farcical train of events is preying on Mr Biswas's mind at the time the passage is written, and so his need to externalise his anger and sense of injustice by writing is reflected there. Seth and Mrs Tulsi are familiar targets in their attempts to interfere with the autonomy of Mr Biswas and his need to feel that his wife and children belong to him rather than to the Tulsis.

The passage also highlights other facets of Mr Biswas's character, particularly his sense of absurdity and his talent for irreverent and facetious writing, which gains a fuller outlet in his job at the *Sentinel* under Mr Burnett. Mr Biswas can never take himself too seriously for long; humour and caricature are his weapons against the oppression he encounters and which the Tulsis personify. We see this in the names he has invented for them like 'the old hen' and 'the little gods', or his later image of Mrs Tulsi when she objects to Anand repeating hymns he has learnt at Sunday school, as a 'Roman cat'. He says comically to Shama: 'I thought a good Christian hymn would remind her of happy childhood days as a baby Roman kitten'. A similar point is made when Mr Biswas compares himself with the holy pundit, Hari, who has a respected position within the Tulsi household. He knows that he could never sustain such a role, just as he cannot share Misir's tragic vision. He observes that he would inevitably be discovered 'in dhoti, top-knot, sacred thread and caste-marks, reading "The Manxman" and "The Atom".'

He finds Misir's rather macbre and ironic story 'puzzling'. It would seem that such an arbitrary and depressing view of life, as expressed by the story, is foreign to Mr Biswas's temperament. He is more optimistic and remains convinced, even after the period at The Chase, that 'some nobler purpose awaited him'. The period at The Chase, although it has involved the acquisition of furniture and other symbols of permanence, has always seemed to him temporary and rather unreal, as though it is still a 'preparation' for life. He feels that he does not look like a shopkeeper, and his true identity still eludes him. This search for identity, which is a central theme in the novel, is shown in his various acts of rebellion, including the one immediately after the passage quoted, when he devotes himself to various absurdities such as growing his nails to an extreme length, or dabbing coloured ointments on his face. These gestures of non-conformity suggest the inner distress which will erupt more forcibly in the breakdown at Green Vale, but also pinpoint, like the scurrilous stories, the frustration that Mr Biswas is feeling – later epitomised in his constant murmurs of 'trap' at Green Vale.

The passage quoted thus points to a number of themes in the novel, chiefly the search for identity with which Mr Biswas is preoccupied, and the way in which he finds relief and refuge in satire. It also reflects traits of character in Mr Biswas's reactions to Misir's story, and his inability to view life in a tragic way. We are also told that he could never devise a story, and this is shown in the novel by his failure to write more than a few lines of his 'Escape' stories except on a few rare occasions. He does compose the prose poem to his mother, and the long letter to the doctor which developed into a 'broad philosophical essay on the nature of man', but his imaginative writings remained confined by his experience and are principally a realm of fantasy to which he can escape. He continues to find comfort and consolation in reading, notably in discovering the 'grotesques' of Dickens which he can identify in the people around him during his latter period at the *Sentinel*, a discovery which he is able to share with his son. His gift for wit and invective is certainly suggested, and displayed in a vivid way elsewhere in the novel with its subtle blend of humour and pathos without the bleakness contained in the story by Misir.

Part 5

Suggestions for further reading

The text

NAIPAUL, V. S.: *A House for Mr Biswas*, Deutsch, London, 1961; the paperback edition published by Penguin Books, Harmondsworth, 1961, is the edition referred to in these Notes.

Other works by V. S. Naipaul

The Middle Passage, Deutsch, London, 1962; Penguin Books, Harmondsworth, 1969, and *An Area of Darkness*, Deutsch, London, 1964; Penguin Books, Harmondsworth, 1968, are particularly useful. It is obviously valuable for students to read other works by V. S. Naipaul, particularly those which are set in Trinidad. All of V. S. Naipaul's works (see Part 1 of these Notes), except his most recent book of essays *The Return of Eva Peron*, Deutsch, London, 1980, are available in Penguin paperback editions.

Critical commentaries

HAMNER, R. D. (ED.): *Critical Perspectives on V. S. Naipaul*, Heinemann, London, 1967. This contains a variety of essays and interviews with Naipaul; the two essays by G. Rohlehr and one by M. Warner-Lewis are of particular interest.

RAMCHAND, K.: *An Introduction to the Study of West Indian Literature*, Nelson, London, 1976. This contains some perceptive comments on the relationship between Mr Biswas and Anand.

THEROUX, P.: *V. S. Naipaul, An Introduction to his Work*, Deutsch, London, 1972.

WALSH, W.: *V. S. Naipaul*, Oliver and Boyd, London, 1973. This contains some interesting comments on the novel.

WHITE, LANDEG: *V. S. Naipaul: A Critical Introduction*, Macmillan, London, 1975.

Cultural and social background

PARRY, J. H. and SHERLOCK, P.: *A Short History of the West Indies*, Macmillan, London, 1956. This provides a useful, basic introduction to the West Indies in a historical context.

AUGIER, F. R.: *The Making of the West Indies*, Longman, London, 1960. This also provides social and economic background information.